MADISON CENTRAL SCHOOL

ESEA TITLE I I
SPECIAL PURPOSE
INCENTIVE GRA

D1201243

John James Audubon

To most Americans the name Audubon means *birds*, drawn in their natural color and setting. Bird lovers check every bird they see against the pictures and notes of the brilliant artist and naturalist of the early 1800's, John James Audubon.

From boyhood it was apparent that the impractical and charming Audubon could not and would not do anything but observe these lovely creatures and paint detailed, lifelike pictures of them. But how, his family fretted, was he to earn a living? His attempts in studies and business were failures. Yet with his faithful wife Lucy standing by him, Audubon eventually realized his life's ambition—the creation and publication of life-size paintings of every bird in America.

MADISON CENTRAL SCHOOL

John James
AUDUBON

by Margaret and John Kieran

Illustrated by Christine Price

ESEA TITLE I I
SPECIAL PURPOSE
INCENTIVE GRANT

Landmark
BOOKS

[Random House   New York]

Copyright 1954 by Margaret and John Kieran

All rights reserved under International and
Pan-American Copyright Conventions

Published in New York by Random House, Inc.
and simultaneously in Toronto, Canada by
Random House of Canada, Ltd.

Library of Congress Catalog Card Number: 54-6269

Manufactured in the U.S.A.

6 466

Contents

Foreword

THE SAGA of John James Audubon has great and everlasting human appeal, because he attained fame and fortune in spite of temperamental handicaps that he strewed in his own path and regardless of a lack of business or diplomatic sense so complete as to astonish and dismay his associates. He furnishes an outstanding example of the success that comes from determination and perseverance in doing exceedingly well that in which one is most interested and talented.

To distill in these few pages the essence of Audubon's history and personality, and to do so with such deft touch and perception, is an accomplishment for which we pay tribute to the skill of Margaret and John Kieran.

JOHN H. BAKER
President, The National Audubon Society

Note to the Reader

All chapter headings are direct quotations from Audubon's Letters or Journals.

Four hundred and thirty-two of the 435 water-color paintings prepared by John James Audubon for his *Birds of America* are owned by the New York Historical Society. Each one measures 39½ by 26½ inches.

The original prints engraved and colored by Havell and Lizars and their assistants may be seen in many museums, libraries and private homes throughout the world. Five such prints are owned by Mr. and Mrs. Kieran.

1

"She was to me a true Mother"

ON A WARM MAY afternoon in 1793, the little town of Nantes in western France was beginning to show the beauty of spring.

The flowers knew it. The birds knew it. And one boy, at least, knew it.

He was Jean Jacques Audubon and he had strayed far away from home so that he could be alone in the woods, discovering with joy the reappearance of a familiar flower or plant or bird.

All day long the sun had been strong; there was so little breeze that the leaves barely stirred. But even so, the boy noticed a movement in the branches above his head, and it was this movement that made his eyes narrow as he watched.

On a second limb, close to the trunk, a

small yellow bill appeared; then a bird's dark head and now, in sharp silhouette, the whole bird. It was a blackbird, known in France and in England, too, as a very fine singer.

Slowly, Jean Jacques raised himself on one elbow in order to get a better view.

"If I am quite still," he thought, "the bird will not notice me. Then I can see how it sings and hops. . . . And when I go home I will draw it just as I remember it."

But he was not thinking of going home quite yet. In fact, if he had his own way he would spend many hours of the day and night in the woods. Even as he was thinking of this a woman's voice sounded.

"Fougère! Fougère!" she said, calling him by his nickname. "See, it will be dark soon and Papa will be home. . . . And you will *not* be home and that will make Papa very angry."

Slowly he noticed a movement in the branches overhead.

Young Audubon frowned. Though he loved his stepmother, he had to admit that it was a nuisance to hear her voice. He would have much preferred to hear the brisk "B-z-z-z-t! B-z-z-z-t!" of a nightjar in the sky overhead, but that would have to wait for another twilight.

Now the stepmother's voice sounded close at hand and she appeared at a turn of the path, puffing a little.

"I don't know what we will do with you, always running away and hiding in the woods. Your sister, Muguet, I find so much more docile."

He got up slowly, brushed the twigs from his coat and said without enthusiasm, "I am coming, Maman. I am coming." Then, quietly to himself, "But I would rather stay."

All the way home she chattered and clucked like a mother hen. *When* would he learn to be on time for meals? *When* would he dress in proper clothes the way other boys did?

They hurried along and luckily arrived at the kitchen garden before Captain Audubon appeared. In just a few moments Fougère had bathed and was ready for supper.

Around the table that night it was a typical family gathering. The Captain sat at the head, looking across candles at his wife. Fougère and his stepsister Muguet were seated quietly on either side.

"And how goes the school work, my son?" the Captain was saying. "The history, now . . . you are learning it well? And the mathematics? You apply yourself here, too?"

Fougère tapped the fine linen tablecloth nervously and gave his stepmother an appealing look.

She shrugged her shoulders. "The boy is no student," she pointed out to her husband. "That is all too apparent."

"But he can *answer me.* . . ." The Captain's voice showed a little anger now.

"Hush," said his wife.

He began again more quietly. "I want to hear, Fougère, that you have given up all that foolishness about straying in the woods and collecting birds' nests and other such nonsense. Any boy of mine is going to amount to something in the world, and it is not by daydreaming in the woods that *this* is accomplished, I can tell you."

Again young Audubon, or Fougère, drummed on the table and said nothing.

But the Captain was a strong-willed man and he could get an answer from a boy of his own as well as from one of his deckhands.

"Will you study now? And *study well* in school?"

"I-I promise. . . . I promise I will *try*, Father."

Then, thankful that grace after meals

served to change the subject, Fougère bowed his head, said "Amen" (a little eagerly, it is true), and excused himself with Muguet.

Out on the terrace they giggled over the way the jelly had trembled when the maid brought it to the table. They giggled, too, at the way Papa's eyebrows seemed to stand right out like a hedgehog's quills when he was angry.

Inside the house there was no giggling, though, for their parents were deep in a conversation regarding the boy's future.

"He is a strange one," they agreed. "He needs careful watching so that he will be a fine man—a good man and one who can earn his own living."

As they talked about this the Captain had a faraway expression in his eyes. He was thinking, no doubt, of his stay in Santo Domingo where young Audubon was born, and where the boy's mother had died not long afterward. Later, the sorrowing Captain had brought the child back to France where Madame Audubon, his stepmother, lavished as much affection on him as though he had been her own son. In fact, the truth is that in her anxiety to show that she was not like the wicked stepmothers of fairy tales, she really spoiled him.

He had his own room, his own nurse, and the finest clothes she could buy.

Soon he had forgotten all about that faraway tropical island.

2

"My Stepmother…completely spoiled me"

IT WAS EASY for Jean Jacques Audubon to feel at home in France.

First of all, there was the house itself to be explored. Up the stairs he went and down the long hall with many closets, then upstairs again to where the servants and his own nurse slept.

On rainy days he and Muguet, the little girl his father had adopted, made up hide-and-seek games that they could play in all the nooks and crannies. But a house is not mysterious forever, and on a sunny day the boy found that it was more fun to wander down the street and see what lay at the end of a crooked lane.

Many, many times his big Haitian nurse

"Come back!" she called. "You are straying too far."

poked in and out of doorways looking for her young charge.

"*Mon Dieu!* He is lost now surely," she would exclaim. "And what will the Captain do to me?" She never felt that she was working for Madame Audubon. It was always "The *Captain* says" or "I will ask the *Captain's* permission."

She became a familiar figure in the street as she called: "Fougère! Come back! You are straying too far away."

It was like calling a bird back to his nest after he had tasted the joy of freedom. Oh, he came. He came. But so slowly!

Once home again the nurse turned him over to Madame Audubon, who petted and pampered him as if he were the only boy in the entire world.

If we remember that France was a troubled country at that time, we can understand a little better why Madame Audubon was so anxious to see that the boy received some joy out of life. The French Revolution was on and the echoes of it sounded in every little village.

Both Fougère's stepmother and father regretted that these troubled times kept him from having a regular schooling.

But he was like any other boy in this respect: it did not make him unhappy at all to find out that he was not able to go to school regularly as young people do today.

For him this meant only one thing: he had all the more time to wander along the banks of the Loire River, quite near his home. All the more time to see what flowers and trees he could discover.

All the more time to watch the birds!

3

"My room exhibited quite a show"

"WHAT DOES Fougère want for his birthday?" asked Captain Audubon of his wife one evening as they sat in the upstairs living room.

She looked up from her embroidery and shook her head. "Such a boy," she said. "All he asks for are pencils and crayons, pencils and crayons."

The Captain frowned, puzzled. "He wants them for his school work?"

"Not at all. . . . Not at all. . . . He wants them for his pastimes . . . for his drawing. The child is like a fiend in drawing. It seems he cannot stop. He goes to the fields and comes home and what does he do? Draw, draw, draw, draw. And now lately, it is always pictures of the birds."

Again the Captain frowned. "Hmmmm. . . . So the lessons are neglected as usual. . . . A little artist, then, we have in the family. I hoped the boy would take to the sea like a man."

His wife drew a long green thread through the piece of cloth as she outlined the stem of a rose. "We cannot *make* them become what we wish, it seems," she observed simply. "The good Lord has His say, also, I suppose . . . as well as the boy himself," she added as an afterthought.

The Captain said nothing for a moment or two. Then he spoke decisively. "I hope you will not encourage this—er—waste of time, my dear. The boy must be made to study mathematics and geography. The other foolishness is only a pastime. I intend to make my boy a student."

Madame Audubon finished the rose as

she said, "He is truly a problem, this boy.
Now if you had only the time to visit his
room and see what he collects you would
understand that his interest in nature is
very, very deep. I thought at first as you
did, that it was a childish fancy. But only
come with me and see what he has there and
you will agree, I think, that his pastime
might be encouraged."

"Not now," said the Captain as he walked
over to his desk. "Some other time when I
have no papers to go over."

He opened the top drawer.

"Two thousand pounds of sugar at——"
he half whispered to himself. And then,
pen in hand, he made some notations in his
ledger. This was the big book that was
known to the servants as the one thing on
Captain Audubon's desk that must not be
touched. In the ledger were the records of

what he had taken to Santo Domingo, how much he had sold it for, and what he had brought back in its place and the price.

On one of his returns to Nantes he was able to spend a few weeks more than usual in port. During this time he seems to have made an effort to become a little better acquainted with his son, for he stopped as Fougère was coming in the terrace door.

"And what is this, my son?" he asked, pointing to an object the boy was holding.

"I think it is the nest of a swallow, Papa. There are no eggs, and I did not see the bird. Still, I think it may be the swallow's nest for I have seen another like this one with a swallow in it."

"And you bring this in from the barnyard? . . . Why is that? . . . What good is it?"

Young Audubon looked down at the floor. It was very hard to explain why the most exciting thing in the world was to go out alone and hunt for birds' nests, or to find the tracks of an unknown animal. He started to stammer as he answered.

"I—I like to see these things . . . to s-see how they are made . . . and then I—I s-save them."

Even to the boy himself it sounded like a weak explanation, but Captain Audubon, remembering what his wife had told him, resolved to try to understand this urge to collect anything to do with birds and flowers and animals.

He took Fougère's hand. "Let us see what you do while I am away," he said gently. "Maman tells me your room is a kind of museum."

Fougère flushed. "It is not tidy," he said. "Wait, Papa!" In a rush of pleading he ran ahead. "I could go and tidy it. I did not know you were coming home today."

But Captain Audubon was impatient now.

"No, no, no," he said. "Tidiness is not as important as *what is there.*"

They walked upstairs and down the hall to the little room at the end where the boy kept his treasures.

The Captain's eyes were wide with astonishment when he stood in the doorway. For all he could see were birds' nests, birds' eggs, drawings of birds, paintings of birds, pressed flowers, pressed leaves, bits of twigs, moss, and lichens. There were other things, too, that no one could identify because they were so old and withered.

All this time the boy was silent. Would his father scold him and tell him to "throw those things away"? Or, worse still, would he laugh at him? That would be too hard to bear.

But this time he was to be surprised, because his father said nothing. He simply

Captain Audubon picked up one of the drawings.

walked over to the table where piles of drawings were scattered and picked one up.

"This sketch, my son," he said. "It is not
bad, really."

"Oh, but it *is*, Papa. It is not the way the
bird looked at all. See how stiff I made the
tail. And how it hangs on like . . . oh, like
a ship's rudder. It was a lovely bird and its
feathers lay flat . . . *so*. . . . See? But I tried
and tried and still I could not seem to make
them lie flat."

He turned to his father suddenly. "This
sketching and painting, can it not be learned
in school, Papa?"

"But of course. There are teachers of
painting in Paris. Indeed people come from
miles around to study with them. But you,
Fougère, you are still too young.

"Moreover," the Captain went on, "Maman tells me that when I am away you do
not study your mathematics or your his-

tory. Perhaps the same things will happen if I send you to Paris to study the drawing, eh?"

But this time there was a twinkle in the good Captain's eye. He remembered other talks he had had with the boy and he knew that Fougère would rather paint than eat his supper.

Picking up another sketch from the cluttered table, the Captain asked, "And what is this?"

His son began talking quickly, excitedly. His eyes sparkled as they always sparkled and always *would* sparkle when he was describing something that he loved.

"It is the sedge sparrow. I worked very hard here. I do not like to draw the bird alone. I like to put it on a branch the way I see it sitting. Also I like to paint in the berries that it eats and sometimes a few leaves because the green is such a nice, soft color."

The Captain listened. Then he walked over to the wastepaper basket. In it were many black-and-white sketches as well as water colors. There were birds, of course, but there were animals, too, and insects.

"And why are these discarded?" he asked.

"They do not please me enough to save," Fougère replied. "They are too stiff and sometimes the color is too strong and sometimes the color is not strong enough."

He felt warm and glowing all over to have his father talking to him almost as an equal. It was the first time this had ever happened . . . the first time the busy Captain had ever listened for more than a few seconds.

In a burst of affection Fougère flung his arms around the Captain's neck. "Paris?" he whispered. "You said one can be taught painting in Paris. Maybe if I am good enough you will send me there?"

It would have been a hard moment for any

father and especially for this one whose heart had been set on having the boy become a naval officer. The Captain looked at his son. Fougère's eyes seemed almost on fire and his look of pleading captivated the man.

"Very good," the Captain said suddenly. "If you apply yourself while I am away on my next journey, you shall go to Paris and study with the greatest teacher I know: Jacques Louis David."

There was a gay family supper that night as Madame Audubon, planning far ahead, discussed the clothing Fougère would take to Paris. Little Muguet begged for a china doll from the big city. But Captain Audubon sat quietly studying the boy, wondering if his decision had been a wise one.

4

"... for dancing I was quite enthusiastic"

"ONE, TWO, THREE, one, two, three, one, two, three."

The dancing instructor was beating time in the music room overlooking the Audubons' country garden at Couëron, not far from their town house in Nantes. It was a beautiful day in early summer and the sunlight poured across the room, bringing into sharp focus a huge cloisonné vase of which Madame Audubon was very proud. The sunlight danced on her oil paintings, too, and on the fragile chairs and tables which made the room such a charming eighteenth-century setting for a dancing lesson.

Little Jean Jacques Audubon pointed one foot ahead, then the other, now bowing to an imaginary partner, now turning around

in the stately movement of the minuet. He
had been born with the gift of music, so
dancing came as naturally to him as
drawing.

The instructor hummed some of Mozart's
music as he continued his measured beat
against the stand. He smiled at the boy.

"Truly you are my most apt pupil," he
said. "Truly I have to show the steps to you
only once and you have them in that quick
mind. Let us go over it just once more for
smoothness. Then we can go on to the steps
of the gavotte."

The morning passed so pleasantly that it
seemed no time at all before the summons to
luncheon was heard.

This was the meal that plump Madame
Audubon especially enjoyed. Here, with
the two children by her side, she could bask
in the dream of the time when they would
be cultured young people. Her thoughts

Young Audubon followed the steps of the dancing master.

would turn to the day when music, dancing, fencing, and all the other accomplishments would have become as casual a part of their lives as bathing or eating.

The children sat on the edges of their

chairs, waiting for the special chicken dish the cook had prepared that day. Seasoned perfectly, it was surrounded by tiny little vegetables just picked from their own kitchen garden.

"Tut, tut now . . . not quite so fast," Madame Audubon warned. "A gentleman eats his food slowly, thus, and talks meanwhile with his luncheon companion."

Jean put his fork down and took a quick breath. "But it's so good," he insisted. "And look. Muguet has hers finished and is asking for still more."

"Hush. Let not one blame the other. Both must be good children," said Madame Audubon. "And both must eat slowly. . . . So."

They watched her as she took small pieces of the chicken on her fork and chewed them painstakingly. "I heard the minuet this morning," she said to the boy. "How did the lesson go?

He finished what he was eating and then said, "Oh, very well. It is fun, this dance. Even if Monsieur did not show me the steps, I think my feet would know how to go. The music almost tells me, it seems."

Muguet was still too busy eating to join in the conversation, but Madame Audubon was so much interested in a report on the morning's progress that she did not notice this.

When the country strawberries and cream were set on the table however, even the mother stopped speaking and the three finished their luncheon in silence.

In silence?

No. Overhead, suddenly, sweetly, came a bird's song that meant only one thing to the boy who turned to listen. Spring was at hand and with it the return of the migrant birds.

"A cuckoo," he said. "The first I've heard this year. . . . My pencil, please,

Maman. I left it over beside you. May I
be excused before grace after meals?"

He was really excited now, so excited that
his ever indulgent stepmother had to say,
"Yes."

When he stood up, he moved slowly to a
place from which he could observe the
singer. Then, outlining the branch of the
tree with a few quick strokes, he began to
draw the bird. As his pencil moved along
he talked softly, half to himself. "The head
not quite so low. His throat quivers as he
sings. . . . Hmmmm. . . . Oh, he has flown
to a lower branch. . . . Then I will draw
him facing me instead of on the side."

What an interesting painting this group
would have made. . . . Madame Audubon
watching him with love and pride, Muguet
peering over his shoulder at the drawing,
and young Audubon himself, fingers tense,
eyes darting from the bird to his paper.

The maid was the only one who showed
no interest. She was too busy wondering if
the family had left enough chicken on the
platter for her luncheon.

When the sketch was finished Madame
Audubon examined it carefully. "You did
well," she said.

But Fougère was not satisfied. He shook
his head. "Only wait until I go to Paris
and study with Monsieur David—" he began, when his mother clapped her hands
over her mouth in dismay.

"Good heavens!" she said. "We sit here
sketching and chattering when you know
your father promised to send you to Paris
only if you studied your school lessons dili-
gently every afternoon. Quick now! Away
with the sketchbook! Let us start with geography and then we can review yesterday's
task in mathematics."

Fougère edged over to her and put his

little hand in hers. "One favor, please, Maman," he begged. "The birds are just coming back and it has been so long since I have had a live model. Only let me sketch this afternoon and I promise I will study my other lessons twice as well tomorrow."

It was always this way. A promise to study tomorrow and tomorrow and tomorrow. For each tomorrow brought even more attractive birds to the trees near by. Birds that seemed to call to him, "See me! Draw me! See me! Draw me!"

Is it any wonder that, upon Captain Audubon's return from this latest sailing trip, there were some tense moments in his son's life?

Fougère waited upstairs until he heard his father calling the two children.

"Now," Captain Audubon said to his wife, *"for the last time* we shall see what they have learned in my absence."

Madame Audubon whispered a little prayer.

The children came downstairs, kissed their father, and waited primly beside him until he told them to be seated.

5

"I preferred going in search of birds' nests"

*T*HE CANDLELIGHT flickered and darted in the breeze that swept through the drawing room. Fougère shivered a little though it was a warm breeze. He clenched and unclenched his fingers nervously as he tried to brace himself for what he felt sure would be the anger of his father.

Maman was there in the rose-brocade chair as usual, her face calm, but her own heart beating rather rapidly.

And Muguet? With her hands folded, she sat in her best muslin dress, her round eyes turned almost flirtatiously toward the colorful Captain.

It was not a long-drawn-out affair, this family gathering. True to his training through the years, Captain Audubon was a man of little talk and swift action. He asked the children to tell what they had learned during his absence.

Muguet ran to the pianoforte and played her latest, her most difficult exercise. When she had finished, the Captain praised her.

"Very good, my child," he said. "I commend you. I can see the result of daily practice there."

He patted her head, and she smiled with delight.

"And Fougère?" he asked anxiously, for on this visit he had high hopes for the boy he had once thought scatterbrained. After all, hadn't that promise of drawing lessons in Paris been held out as a reward for daily study?

Fougère began talking rapidly about his collection of birds' nests. "The ones you liked, Papa . . ." he reminded him.

"Yes, yes . . . Fine . . . But what about your mechanical drawing? Let me see what you have done there. And let me hear you play the violin."

The boy could only hang his head.

Poor Madame Audubon. She must have felt guilty, too, remembering how she had encouraged him in his dancing and in his fencing, remembering, too, how she herself had neglected to prod him into working on his other lessons. But she kept her eyes upon the floor because she knew the Captain's temper.

There were a few more pointed questions, a few more halting and unsatisfactory answers from the boy, and the Captain told him abruptly that he was excused and might go to bed.

In a journal written much later, Audubon says he remembers his father's humming a little tune in a preoccupied way.

The Captain was thinking of a plan which he carried into effect the next morning, and *early* the next morning. For it was just after dawn that the boy was awakened, told to dress and pack a little trunk.

Where was he going? He had no idea. The stern-faced Captain said not a word but hustled him into the carriage, making sure that the trunk was fastened securely in back and that the boy's violin case was at his feet. They entered the carriage silently.

The Captain did not even look at his son, but instead took from his bag a book which he started to read. Indeed he scarcely stopped reading until they arrived at their destination, a naval school at Rochefort.

It was a hard and a memorable experience for a boy not yet seventeen. The discipline was strict there, in sharp contrast to Madame Audubon's easy ways. Young Audubon was a stranger and a shy and sen-

They hustled into a carriage and dashed off.

sitive one. But he was not too shy to plan
his escape from the jail-like school. He had
been there only a short time when he
jumped out of a window and started to run
away.

A short-lived escape it proved to be,
however, because he was caught almost as
soon as he could draw a breath of freedom.

When the authorities communicated with
Captain Audubon about his son's latest es-
capade, the worried father gave up at last.

"He is different," he conceded, "and I must face it."

When young Audubon was home from the naval school, we can picture him waiting, half frightened, to see what would happen next.

He gave a shout of joy when his father told him the news. "We have decided to send you to Paris to study art."

The house must have echoed with young Audubon's glee.

"You will see," he said to his father. "You will be proud of me some day."

Swift preparations were made.

He was in Paris before he could catch his breath.

6

"The lessons I received from David proved all-important"

IN LOOKING back over the story of Audubon's youth, many people have said that he was a flighty boy, unable to put his mind on the thing at hand. They point to his experience in Paris as an example of this.

His anxiety to study there was great when he had first heard of the artist, Jacques Louis David. But then what happened?

After he had been with David only a little while, he became bored by the stiff white statues he was asked to copy. This type of basic instruction, used by many art schools today, seemed dull to young Audubon. He wanted color . . . bright color.

Day after day in the classroom he frowned as his teacher, a fine one, pointed

out the modeling on a head of Julius Caesar,
for example. He drew attention to the
strong jaw, which the students must indi-
cate with a swift, sure stroke of charcoal,
and to the neck so muscular and powerful.
While the other students hunched eagerly
over their easels, drawing here, erasing
there, Audubon seems to have had a little
scorn for their earnestness.

Very often his gaze would wander out
the window to where a stray pigeon had
caught his eye. Now there was something
worth painting! Even though it was only
gray, or gray and black-and-white, there
were gradations of color that would allow
some delicacy in his brush strokes, some
play of tone. And most important of all,
he thought, his subject was alive!

Those daydreams were always interrupted by Monsieur David.

"You are not interested in the subject

It was very boring to draw those stiff white statues.

matter today, Jean?" he said one afternoon
when the shadows were growing long and
the studio had become a little dim. "You
are not interested in the fine head we are
working on? See how Paul beside you
works and works on the nose so that it will
come *out* and on the cleft in the chin so
that it will go *back*. That is the basis of all
your drawing no matter how long you study
and how famous you may become."

How famous you may become.

Young Audubon's eyes brightened and
he pricked up his ears. For he *would* become famous some day, perhaps. Not because he drew black-and-white sketches of
whole plaster heads, though. Not because
he worked in a dim studio in Paris.

No, perhaps success would come because
he would paint birds in full color. Lovely,
lively birds. His birds would not be the
stuffed ones a person could see in a mu-

seum. They would look as if they had just lighted on a branch, or as if they were swooping through the air.

Monsieur David saw that his pupil was not paying any attention to his short lecture. He walked wearily over to the candelabra and lit one after the other slowly.

"The importance of working in black-and-white is clearly seen at this time of day," he was saying, "when the light grows poor. If we had been using oils or pastels our colors would have changed. Naturally they would become yellow because of the candlelight. When we regarded our work the next day everything would have a sickly, unrealistic look."

But the light had little effect on charcoal on white paper and the students went ahead eagerly, hardly noticing that soon it would be time for supper. All the students, that is, except the slim, dreamy-eyed boy who hated to admit to himself that his father had been right after all. Yes, he was tiring very quickly of the strict discipline his Paris art course imposed.

A few more weeks of this, a few more attempts to capture a likeness from a statue, and young Audubon decided he could not go on for another day. Picture his humiliation as he returned to his home.

From Muguet: "I thought you were going to bring me a doll and become a great painter."

From his stepmother: "Home again, my son? . . . Not a student yet, eh? . . . You do not even like the painting as you thought you would?"

His father: "Come into my study, son. Now at last we must have a serious talk. You are no longer a child. In a few years you will be a man. Come now, if you

please. Tell Maman we will be late for dinner and they must not wait."

The boy walked slowly behind his father,
who closed the door as soon as they had entered the study. The walls were lined with
books, books, books, and the unhappy Fougère wished with all his heart that he might
become one of them so that he would not
have to listen to the lecture he knew he
was about to receive.

But it was too late now. It was something that simply must be faced. Squirm-
ing nervously in the huge carved chair, he
waited for the sound of his father's stern
voice.

7

"It was my greatest pleasure to observe nature"

THE INTERVIEW was a short one. Both father and son knew that it was bound to be. After all, whatever had to be said had been said many times before. Jean Jacques was no longer a child. Soon he would be out of his teens and approaching an age at which a youth should either be in the army or out of it, earning his own living.

The year was 1803. France, in a turmoil at the time, was not an inviting prospect for the young man, nor was it a place in which his father would like to have seen him remain. Napoleon was recruiting young Frenchmen for campaigns that would not end until twelve years later, at Waterloo!

America, now! That was a different story.

Captain Audubon had property in Pennsylvania, farm lands he had bought and leased on one of his stopovers from Santo Domingo. At that time it was being managed by a Quaker couple—the William Thomases—but like many another father, Captain Audubon would have preferred to see his own son looking after his property. What does not seem to have occurred to him was that his son would show no more interest in mathematics and business in America than he had shown at home.

No matter. The decision was made.

And in the autumn the amateur naturalist who had now passed his eighteenth birthday set sail for the New World.

It was a new world in every sense.

Picture him in the strange land, walking from where he landed in New York City to

Greenwich, Connecticut, in order to cash a
letter of credit his father had given him.
Walking had always been his delight, and
on the way he saw many new birds and
heard many new bird notes. Then he was
dealt a sharp blow. He was stricken with
a kind of fever that would have caused his
death if two kind Quaker ladies had not
nursed him back to health.

When he was well enough to travel again
he pushed anxiously south because he was
eager to establish himself at his father's
farm, called Mill Grove. This was a lovely
rambling estate in Pennsylvania, not far
from Philadelphia.

The farmhouse itself pleased him. It
was a two-story affair built of stone which
had been dug from the surrounding country. The location, too, had great charm.
The Perkiomen River rushed along through
cherry, hemlock, and elm trees. No won-

der young Audubon fell in love with the place as soon as he saw it. No wonder he barely deposited his small trunk before he was out exploring the countryside.

If he had been presented with a map of the United States, it is unlikely that he could have put his finger on any part of it that would have satisfied him as completely as this fine rolling country did. One might walk for a few hundred yards through neat little farmyards and then, suddenly, heavily wooded areas bordered the land. The woods were quite unspoiled by man, which meant that birds and other wild creatures were there in abundance.

One day as he ambled along the river's edge he found a cave.

This discovery is an important one in the story of American ornithology—the science of birds—because it marked a beginning in bird banding. Today bird banding

is familiar to many people all over the
world. But listen to Audubon's account of
how it was first done. He had discovered
the cave as a phoebe's nesting place.

"I fixed a light silver thread on the leg
of each," he wrote, "loose enough not to
hurt the part, but so fastened that no ex-
ertions of theirs could remove it."

Then, to his great delight, next spring he
found several of the birds with that little
ring around the leg. This proved that the
migratory instinct, which even today puz-
zles naturalists, had brought these birds
right back to the same spot on the river's
edge.

How he loved that cave!

He made it an actual room, a sort of study
complete with his books, pencils, and paper.
Some of his early drawings of birds were
made there from live or dead models.

Naturally he preferred to sketch a bird in

"I fixed a silver thread on the leg of each," he said.

flight, or as it appeared on the branch of a tree. But if you have ever watched a bird for more than a few seconds you must have noticed that its quick motion is almost impossible to catch with pencil or brush. A warbler darts and flits and turns . . . and vanishes. Though most of the larger birds move a little more slowly, they too fly away when an artist is just about to finish a delicate stroke on beak or claw.

With his zeal for drawing growing more urgent than ever, young Audubon decided to collect birds with his gun so that he would have specimens in hand when he began to draw them. In this way he would be sure that his drawings and paintings were correct in every detail. At that time there were no museum collections such as those that are available to modern bird artists for study.

It is important to understand this. Otherwise we might get a false picture of young Audubon. We might think: "How could he say he loved birds and then shoot them?"

It was a question of loving them so much that he selected and shot a few—male, female, and young birds if necessary—so that he would have perfect models for his magnificent paintings.

In this pleasant way he spent a great part of the first year in America, roaming the fields and forests, watching the birds, shooting those he needed, and drawing day and night.

8

"I measured five feet ten and one half"

"Look! There goes that dashing young Frenchman!"

It was one of the women at a nearby farmhouse who had been watching Audubon for some months now and already had decided that he might be a good "catch" for her youngest daughter.

But at the moment Audubon was not interested in social life. There was too much to see! And not enough time in which to see it.

Yet it was impossible for such an attractive young man to be left alone long, and soon he was really swept into a rush of dances and skating parties and musicales that made him the toast of the neighborhood. He loved clothes at this period of his life and afterwards remarked that he attached a foolish importance to them. Remember, though, that he was imaginative and artistic and so, no doubt, felt he must play the role of a young French blade to a "T."

He was slim and graceful, a fine dancer and skater. No one could glide over the ice as quickly as he. But apparently he entered into all these neighborhood affairs with only half a heart. His real interest was in following the daily routine of a naturalist.

He had so little feeling for making a show of neighborliness that he neglected to return a call that a Mr. William Bakewell made at his home. The Bakewell property adjoined Mill Grove and very likely the owner of the next door property thought it would be the gracious thing to pay his respects to the young stranger from over the seas.

He was swept into a rush of dances and parties.

Audubon says in his journal later that he
was neglectful about returning the call until one day his good breeding asserted itself
and he walked toward Fatland Ford, as the
neighboring estate was called.

It was a beautiful residence with huge
white columns supporting the front, and a
lawn that rolled almost down to the river.

He was shown into the parlor and told
that Mr. Bakewell was not at home but that
his daughter, Miss Lucy, would receive him.

Here in Audubon's words is an account
of the meeting. It is from a letter written
many years later to his sons:

"Well do I recollect the morning, and
may it please God that I may never forget
it . . . the first time I entered Mr. Bakewell's dwelling. It happened that he was
absent from home, and I was shown into a
parlor where only one young lady was
snugly seated at her work by the fire. . . .

There I sat, my gaze riveted, as it were, on the young girl before me who, half working, half talking, essayed to make the time pleasant to me. Oh! may God bless her! It was she, my dear sons, who afterward became my beloved wife, and your Mother."

We can imagine that she was just as suddenly taken by this dashing young Frenchman of whom she must have heard intriguing reports. Who could dance as he could? Who could skate so well? And who could play on the violin with such a touch?

"Love at first sight" is a phrase that people are apt to laugh at a little, but in the case of John and Lucy it seems apt.

Their meetings became more and more frequent. Even though she had to admit he was not the steadiest businessman in the world she was convinced he would be steady in his love for her.

9

"He (Dacosta) was a ... wretch!"

" D ID YOU hear the news, Mr. Audubon?"

It was the excited voice of William Thomas, tenant at Mill Grove, and the tone of urgency in his question made young Audubon put down his pencil. He had been working on the beak of a sparrow hawk and was a little annoyed by the interruption.

"The news?" he said slowly. He held his drawing away to get a better view of the outline. "What news is this?"

Thomas rushed in, pulled up a stool, and sat down with a thump.

"Lead ore!" he shouted. "They've discovered it again at Mill Grove. We can make a fortune!" This was in 1804. Actually the excitement in his voice was all out of proportion to the importance of what he was saying. For the discovery had been made many years before and not much had come of it. Besides, in this rediscovery Thomas and Audubon were not the only ones involved. A Francis Dacosta had bought an interest in the farm and had been appointed as a sort of guardian of young Audubon.

The two did not get along well. From the moment of their meeting it was a clash of temperaments which was never smoothed out.

From Audubon's tale of their encounters Dacosta was an out and out scoundrel. Dacosta, no doubt, was constantly enraged by the young naturalist's lack of business sense, so his side of their disagreements puts a different light on things.

All their differences, all their quarrels, whether about the overrated importance of the lead ore or about something else, came to a head when the youth was convinced that Dacosta was trying to ruin the business.

"I had to go to France to expose him to my father to get rid of him," said Audubon. Not only was he convinced that the fellow was a swindler, but he was also angry because Dacosta objected to his proposed marriage to Lucy Bakewell.

No wonder Audubon hurried back to Nantes in 1805 like a small boy, flinging his cares at a father's feet.

The father listened to him, in order to let him relieve his pent-up anger, no doubt, but there is no record that he moved Dacosta from his post. In fact, letters written by Captain Audubon prove that he, too, was anxious to postpone his son's marriage, until he could at least get some information about the bride-to-be. Times were not what they had been, and it was important that his son marry a young lady of property.

But these problems were put aside temporarily while young Audubon led a carefree life, roaming the French countryside once more. By the greatest stroke of good luck he formed a friendship with Dr. Charles Marie d'Orbigny who lived quite near Captain Audubon's country place at Couëron.

The doctor was a perfect companion since he, too, was interested in everything to do with the out-of-doors. He loved to hunt, he loved to fish, and he loved to walk out and examine everything from a tiny insect to the largest hawk on wing. It was without doubt the most valuable contact of Audubon's youth so far as shaping his life interest is concerned.

They collected every bird and Audubon drew them all. Many of the books that tell of this friendship devote little space to a description of the walks taken by the two men, and that is unfortunate.

The two men roamed the French countryside together.

Still, anyone with an imagination can picture the friends starting out at dawn, with some bread and cheese in a pack already equipped with pencils and a sketching pad. These things, plus the enthusiasm with which every naturalist greets a new day, were all they needed.

No wonder Audubon looked on this as one of the happiest times of his entire life.

But he knew that it must soon end because
there was always the business of Mill Grove
in the back of his mind and the thought of
Lucy Bakewell in the foreground.

So sailing to America was the next move
with Ferdinand Rozier, the son of an old
friend of his father's. Captain Audubon
had arranged that the two should be business partners, so they shipped together on
the brig *Polly* from Nantes, April 12, 1806.
After an exciting trip during which they
were boarded, searched, and robbed by the
crew of a British privateer, they landed in
New York on May 28th.

The young men went on to Mill Grove
where Audubon learned that the mining of
lead ore on his farm would not be profitable.
Shortly thereafter he sold the Audubon interests in the farm to Dacosta and left Mill
Grove for good. He was sorry to leave the
farm but glad to be through with Dacosta.

10

"My Beloved Lucy who . . . loves me"

*H*ERE he was in America for the second time in his life.

He was twenty-one years old.

Now to the business at hand! Put the birds and those bird walks behind you, Mr. Audubon, he may have said to himself. You are a man and you must manage your father's affairs. The life of a merchant is a respectable one. You have a quick mind and a pleasing way of meeting people. So, the sooner the drawing paper and the crayons are hidden in the closet, the closer to the day you will be able to ask Miss Lucy Bakewell to be your wife.

At last Audubon made up his mind to go into business. He attached himself to Lucy's uncle in New York and stayed there almost a year learning something about the sale of linens, laces, gloves, wines, and firearms, as well as coffee and sugar.

Then he decided to go into trade with Rozier in Kentucky.

His father must have been pleased to think that the young man was settling down at last, even though his only reason for turning to business was to make Lucy his wife. This is what young Audubon wrote to his father April 24, 1807:

". . . About three weeks ago I went to Mill Grove and had the pleasure of seeing there my Beloved Lucy who constantly loves me and makes me perfectly happy. I shall wait for thy Consent and the one of my good Mamma to marry her. Could thou but see her and thou wouldst I am sure, be pleased of the prudency of my choice."

The prudency of his choice! In all the stories you can read about great men and

He learned about selling linens, laces and gloves.

small, it is doubtful that you will ever read of one whose wife was such a helpmate in the truest sense of the word.

You might never have heard of Audubon today if it were not for her. She loved the young, happy-go-lucky painter and had a faith in him that never wavered, even when they had scarcely enough to eat. She *believed* that he would become great.

That belief is without doubt the thing that spurred him on to the greatness he at last attained.

But think of the way the neighbors must have talked to her before she married.

"My dear Lucy, you are mad, quite mad! Jean Jacques is charming, it is true, but what kind of husband will he make? A girl must be practical, after all, and do you think he is steady? Oh, I know he does not drink or gamble. But can he earn a living? Has he a way with figures?"

A way with figures? Not on ledgers. Only if they were the flying figures of birds as they soared above him. Lucy knew this. But never mind. She loved him for what he was and for what she knew he would become.

They were married April 5, 1808.

His assets? Many drawings of birds, a great desire to draw more . . . and Lucy.

11

"I shot, I drew, I looked on nature only"

"*L*ook out there!"

One of the passengers in the honeymooners' coach was crying out a warning as the carriage went around a bad curve in the Allegheny Mountains. Suddenly the carriage turned over, tossing out Lucy and her husband. Audubon picked himself up quickly, for he was always in top physical form, but his wife was a little slower.

"My darling, are you hurt?" he cried.

Between the confusion of straightening the carriage and getting her to her feet again, there wasn't time to find out the extent of her injuries. She made light of them anyway and it was only a few days later that the black and blue marks showed. But that was such a small matter when the im-

portant thing was always before them . . .
their trip to Louisville, Kentucky, to establish a home there.

Nowadays, of course, hundreds and thousands of miles mean nothing when one
starts to travel. But in those early days a
trip to Louisville was almost like a trip to
the moon. It took the Audubons twelve
days by carriage and flatboat, twelve days
through wildly beautiful country.

Louisville was their choice because young
Audubon had already explored the terri-
tory. In fact, he had tended store with
Rozier there and had decided that the people and surroundings would make settling
in Louisville a pleasant and profitable business.

Poor Audubon! Things always looked
rosy to him until the bills started coming in.
And even then, tomorrow was another day.
He did not change when he opened the

store in Louisville. When things looked
black, he was sure the next day would bring
good sales of grain and cutlery and shot
pouches and fruit. In the meantime, the
woods were always inviting.

"But how can you leave the store?" Lucy
wanted to know. Time and again she would
ask him this question as she saw him getting his horse. He would kiss her and point
down the road.

"Rozier, my good partner, will tend to
things while I seek more customers inland,"
was his usual answer.

And Lucy would shake her head. Too
often he had returned from these side trips
only to have to report the loss of his pocketbook.

His explanation was always charming.
"I don't know how it happened, my dear
Lucy," he would begin. "I had had con-
siderable success on this venture, selling

"But how can you leave the store?" Lucy would ask.

more than I dreamed of . . . all that grain
and several knives. Then, suddenly . . ."

"Yes?" Lucy would say anxiously.

"Suddenly I heard a strange, sweet note
overhead. I stopped instantly, not being
able to tell what bird it was. Another call
and I saw it light at the top of a tree. I
brought it down with my gun. The day

was so beautiful . . . clear and sunny. As
I look back now I think I must have pulled
out my pocketbook with my sketch pad, for
alas, I have not seen the pocketbook since.
But no tears," he went on sternly, "for see
. . . my sketch of the rose-breasted grosbeak."

"It . . . it is very fine," she would say as
she tried to hide a little sob. She did love
him so, and she understood his strange nature which made it actually impossible for
him to pay any attention to practical mat-
ters when there were birds around to be
drawn.

But after all, a pretty picture of a pretty
bird would not pay the grocery bill, even
though a story has come down to us that he
once exchanged an original painting for a
much needed pair of shoes.

And then, of course, there were the times
he did portraits of young ladies in order to
earn enough money to buy food for his

family. These uncertain sources of income were not the sort of things to which Lucy was accustomed. After all, she had been brought up in a family that had not only all the necessities of life but many of its luxuries, too. She was used to servants and pretty clothes. Most important of all, she was used to the feeling of security that a regular weekly income brings.

But something about this madcap husband of hers made her believe in him. No doubt she worried when he was away and wondered whatever would become of them, but when he came home his enthusiasm and his tenderness, too, won her completely.

Then, without warning, on a cool March day in 1810 something happened that influenced the whole course of their lives.

12

"Alexander Wilson called upon me"

ONE DAY a sandy-haired Scot turned up
in town.

His name was Wilson . . . Alexander Wilson . . . and by the oddest kind of coinci-
dence he had hit, some years earlier, upon
the idea of drawing all the birds of North
America. Indeed, the first volume of the
Wilson series had already been published.

He and Audubon had never met but now,
dramatically, their paths crossed. They com-
pared drawings, exchanged some natural history information, and parted. Wilson was
no doubt annoyed that he was no longer the
only one in the field, and Audubon himself
felt a bit surprised at finding he had a rival.

The meeting was a very brief one . . . Wilson stayed in town only a few days. Yet

The tiny warbler reminded him of his boyhood.

it was important because of the fact that Audubon was becoming more and more convinced that his great work was to be the publication of *life-size paintings of every North American bird.* This was an even more ambitious project than the one Wilson was undertaking.

As usual, Lucy was right by her husband's side with encouraging words.

"You can do it," she told him excitedly. "You have great talent and great energy. You were not meant to be a shopkeeper.

You must keep getting more specimens.
You must keep painting."

This was what he wanted to hear, and he
was off the next day at sunrise and many,
many days after that. Even his deep affection for their first child Victor, born a year
before, in 1809, did not distract him.

Sometimes as he lay quietly in the woods
waiting for a warbler to appear, he felt like
a little boy again at Nantes. It almost
seemed as if he could hear his stepmother
calling: "Come home, Fougère! It is time
for supper."

But the birds were different here. Such
variety, such color, and so many of them!
The Audubons were living in a wonderful
section for watching the birds travel north
and south, and soon the young naturalist's
portfolio was bulging with water colors, pastels, and rough pencil sketches of every bird
he could discover.

13

"I seldom passed a day without drawing a bird"

"*H*ow do you know what kind of branch to put in as a background for the oriole?" Lucy asked her husband one day as he sat outside the house, his water colors at hand, his sketch pad as usual before him.

"I watch, my dear," he replied. "I watch closely every minute of my time in the woods. There is nothing that I do not notice. The day is not long enough when I am close to nature. Never have I seen such birds as are around Louisville. All of them are not known to me, by any means. The warblers dazzle me in the spring and confuse me in the fall. But *I will draw them.*"

He told her of the black-crowned night herons and the wood ducks that looked al-

most like painted toys. He told her too about
the sound of a bittern that he first thought
was an old-time wooden pump. There were
woodpeckers and barred owls. There were
all the birds that are familiar to us today,
birds we can see in his famous paintings as
well as on the Audubon charts that are
printed in his memory.

Lucy sat mending a woolen sock as he
poured out to her the adventures he had had
in the woods.

It was not enough, you see, for him to observe the birds, to see them feeding or preen-
ing or soaring above him. He must know
just exactly how the feathers folded, one
above the other, how the wings lay close to
the bodies, how the beaks were formed.

During these days, there were the usual
business reverses which once became so serious that Lucy was obliged to take a position
as governess.

Often he walked for miles through rain-drenched fields.

Never mind, they would eat! And Audubon could go on painting.

That is why his gun was always by his side. To capture the actual bird, to put it on his drawing board and to measure every feature, that was what excited him most. The ambition to paint the full life-size series of every bird of America had seized his imagination so that he could think of little else.

For too long he had been dabbling in painting and woodsy daydreaming. For too long he had seen the reproachful looks of his family as he proved that he was not a businessman. Now, at last, he set his jaw and made a resolution. Nothing would stop him from becoming great.

From this time on the story of Audubon's life is a really thrilling tale of singleness of purpose. There were no hardships too extreme for him . . . walking miles in his bare feet when his shoes had worn out, tramping in rain-drenched fields, or wading through stagnant swamps. All these inconveniences were as nothing if he came back with his booty. Maybe it would be an indigo bunting, that true-blue songster that he painted with such love. Maybe it would be the huge wild turkey, one of the most famous of his magnificent series.

Whatever the specimen, Lucy was happy when she saw him returning with it. Busy over a huge kettle in the kitchen, she breathed a prayer of thanks that he would be occupied the next day, feverishly at work on a sketch and later a painting.

14

"Hunting, Fishing, Drawing occupied my every moment"

"If I were jealous I should have a bitter time of it, for every bird is my rival," Lucy wrote to her sister one day when her husband was miles away on a hunting trip.

A hunting trip meant that he was hunting birds, of course, because by this time Audubon was like a man on fire. He thought of nothing but his Great Work. Lucy had to remind him when meals were ready or he would have stayed over his drawing board day and night, painting, tearing up that painting, starting another, making corrections. Then finally he could put the huge sheet of paper away until another day.

Like any true artist he was never satisfied with the finished product.

He studied each bird with the greatest care.

"The Blackburnian warbler I did at Fatland Ford," he said, "I must work over a
little. The bird is not so bad, but the flowers . . . the phlox . . . can stand a little polishing. They are too stiff as I have them now
painted."

He held it away from him.

Lucy did not agree. "It is very delicate,"
she said. "I can almost smell the perfume."

"But see," he pointed out, "here the out-

line should be a little less sharp so that the
bird will stand out."

She nodded and watched him proudly as
he worked painstakingly over every tiny
detail.

He had made great strides in his drawing
technique. And remember that he was
practically self-taught. He had to work out
his own problems with no teacher at his side
to help smooth the way.

At first he was chiefly concerned with
obtaining an accurate likeness of the bird . . .
the exact size, the exact colors, the exact position in flight or at rest. For this he sometimes had to wait months because he needed
not only the male bird from which to work
but the female and often the young as well.
Occasionally he would take a dead bird apart
to see just how the head and jaw were con-
structed, so that each line he drew could be
true to nature.

What fascinated him almost more than anything else was the task of getting a life-like expression in the eyes . . . that frightened and suspicious look a bird has when human beings come near. This Audubon did by sharp highlights, a trick he could have learned at art school, no doubt, but one that he had nevertheless developed alone.

After he was sure that his drawing was accurate, he went on with the task of arranging the bird and the background in an artistic composition. It was not enough to copy nature, he must at times improve upon it.

Look at his painting of the pileated woodpecker, that bold and beautiful bird whose bill *rat-tat-ting* against a tree sounds like a man chopping wood. He pictured these birds against a background of wild grapes. The rich purple-blue of the fruit makes a lovely contrast for the red crests on the birds' heads.

By this time he had learned to paint the wood of trees in that soft brown tone he knew so well from daily observation. Backgrounds, too . . . soft fleecy clouds or distant hills . . . were no longer the difficult subjects they had once been.

All those days of "wasted time" in the woods were beginning to show results.

People—at least a few—were looking at him with a little more respect. Instead of thinking of him as that happy-go-lucky Frenchman who would rather watch birds than count change, they called him "Mr. Audubon," or even "Mr. Audubon, the artist."

It had taken years of observation and notation, but now there was a chance that his work might become known. Each day, each week, and each month swelled that huge portfolio of paintings.

But what good would four hundred or

more pictures of the birds of America be if
he could not sell them?   And how *could* he
sell them?   Who could afford to buy them?

He looked at Lucy, who was always at
hand when a new problem came up.   "I'll
have to work as a merchant a little while
longer," he told her, "and save enough to
pay my way to Philadelphia.   Surely there
are men of taste and wealth there who
would be interested in my paintings."

15

"I bid Rozier farewell"

"*T*OOT-TOOT. *Toot-toot! Toot-toot!*"

The thin tin trumpet of a flatboat sounded her arrival near a port on the Ohio River. It was the big event of the day in those pioneer times. The big event of the month, perhaps!

Aboard the flatboat on this day was the slim young Frenchman, his hair falling in ringlets around his face. He wore rough clothes, for he was living the life of a backwoodsman now. Hunter's knife and double-barreled rifle were almost his most important possessions. But as he turned around to get a better view of the shoreline, his companions noticed a little tin box strapped to his back. In it were drawings and water colors. Strapped to his back, too, were his flute and fiddle. Oh, the days of his journey were never long while he could paint and turn up a tune. But now the flatboat had reached its destination!

Rozier and Audubon had agreed that they could no longer make a success of their store in Louisville and they had decided to push farther south. Henderson, Kentucky, was their goal this time. It was a tiny community of about 150 people, but the two young merchants had been told that it was a thriving settlement and that a country store would do very well there.

They had been in town only a short while when they found out how badly they had been misinformed. The whole section was composed of only a few rude log cabins, and the people seemed to want nothing but whiskey and gunpowder. They showed no interest in the laces and silks that Audubon and his partner had for sale.

This was very discouraging, but since Henderson had not worked out as they planned, they decided to try their luck at a place they had heard good reports of—St. Genevieve, Missouri. This journey proved that Audubon, in spite of his daydreaming, was made of stern stuff when it came to facing the hardships of wild river travel down the Ohio and up the turbulent Mississippi.

The trip was begun during a thaw, when their boat was in constant danger of being dashed apart by huge blocks of ice. They had to lash logs to the boat to protect it from what must have seemed like small icebergs. Edging carefully close to shore, they poled their way along at a snail's pace, for the current was very strong.

But the chances are that if Audubon were alive today he would not even remember the danger and the hardships of this trip. There is just one thing that would recall the whole

That was his first glimpse of the great bald eagle.

adventure to him. It signaled his first glimpse of that magnificent bird, the bald eagle. Let the ice come dangerously near the boat! Let their supply of food dwindle as it did!

He would still have something to make this trip a shining one. And for a less dramatic recollection he could recall glimpses of chickadees, a blue-winged teal, meadowlarks, and Canada geese.

Rozier, a much keener businessman than Audubon, soon found St. Genevieve to his

liking. He proposed that they settle there,
for even a short stay showed him that they
would get good prices for their wares. But
something about the place didn't please
Audubon. If he were thinking only of himself, perhaps he would have agreed to remain, but it struck him that Lucy would not
be happy in that town.

He decided to break with Rozier and go
back to his wife on foot. The trip by boat
down the Ohio and up the Mississippi had
taken two months, so we can only imagine
how long it took him to get home as he wan-
dered through unfamiliar forests.

For food, his gun could always supply him
with rabbits, and then there were Indians
who sometimes offered him a venison stew.
One night, in seeking shelter at a log cabin,
he had a close call when a friendly Indian
warned him by gestures that he was about
to be scalped.

According to his own hair-raising account he escaped just in time, and the adventure made a good story to tell Lucy when he finally reached home.

After all, this last trip had been more successful than most, for he had done fairly well at St. Genevieve. Now, back at Henderson where he had the help of a dependable young clerk named John Pope, he returned to his great passion—roaming the woods and sketching birds.

Of course by this time Audubon had become a sort of curiosity to all the neighbors and friends. They could not help liking him with his easy way of talking and his gift for music and dancing. At the same time, they were more than a little puzzled by his personality.

What kind of man was this who, it was said, would go away from home for months at a time, hunting? Oh, if he were hunting deer they would have understood it, but hunting little birds!

They shook their heads.

All kinds of stories grew up around him, some of them based on fact and others just manufactured because he lent himself to such fables.

Maybe he was the Lost Dauphin. After all, he had lived in France at the time of that famous disappearance. And he never denied the rumor. Maybe, even if he were not of royal birth, he was a genius of some kind. A genius at art, perhaps, or natural history, or both.

These rumors do not seem to have disturbed him at all. He continued to watch in the woods. He continued to draw.

16

"My business abandoned me"

BUT AUDUBON had a wife and child.   Since
he had broken with Rozier, he was out of
business and he had very little money.   In
fact, the Audubons did not even have a home
of their own.   Fortunately their friend, Dr.
Adam Rankin, who was a well-to-do resident
of Henderson, invited them to stay at his
home, Meadow Brook Farm, until they could
find a place for themselves.

Possibly many of Audubon's unhappy experiences in business were his own fault, but
some of them were beyond his control.   For
instance, his next business venture was a
partnership with his brother-in-law, Thomas
Bakewell.   They set up as commission merchants, planning to sell pork and flour to the
overseas trade.   But no sooner had Bakewell

opened an office for the firm in New Orleans than the War of 1812 broke out. That put an end to overseas trade and eventually to the firm of Audubon & Bakewell, too.

However, Audubon had received some money due him from Rozier and had opened a little general store in Henderson. Victor Audubon was now three years old and on November 30, 1812, he was presented with a baby brother, John Woodhouse Audubon. The growing family managed to live for some years on the slim profits from the general store.

The profits might have been larger if Audubon had paid strict attention to business, but he now believed more than ever that the most important thing in his life was to complete his drawings of the native birds of North America. So he spent more time in the woods and over his drawing board than behind the counter of his general store.

The business limped along. The Audubons had a roof over their heads, comfortable clothes on their backs, and good food on the table. If Audubon didn't make money, he at least "held his own" for a period of five years in Henderson. At the same time he was adding, day by day, to his knowledge of birds and to his collection of drawings of native species. During this time he received a sharp blow when rats destroyed hundreds of his sketches.

In the spring of 1817 Audubon entered into a partnership with Thomas Bakewell and Thomas W. Pears for the purpose of building a steam sawmill and gristmill at a cost of $15,000. Apparently most of the money was supplied by Audubon and where or how he obtained it is something of a mild mystery. Perhaps some of it was money owed him by Rozier and others, including Dacosta. In any case, the four-story mill,

65 feet long and 45 feet wide, rose on the
bank of the Ohio at Henderson and was the
smoke-belching sensation of the region.

Corn and wheat came to the mill to be
ground, and trees from the forests near by
furnished logs that were cut by the whirling
saws. Business was brisk at the outset, and
it seemed that Audubon's financial affairs
were at last improving. But the crude steam
engine at the mill broke down repeatedly.
Pears became discouraged and sold out his
interest in the venture to Thomas Bakewell
and Audubon. The mill chugged only now
and then. No profits were produced. Debts
began to pile up.

Instead of growing rich, Audubon was in
financial difficulties again. However, in the
thick of his troubles with what he later called
"the infernal mill," he had a visitor at Henderson whose engaging personality and odd
behavior lightened the gloom temporarily.

It was in the late summer of 1818, and the visitor was a brilliant but odd scientist named Rafinesque.

Constantine Samuel Rafinesque, born thirty-five years earlier of a French father and a Greek mother, was a bald, bent, odd-looking man with flashing eyes, a long thin beard, and queer clothes. When he landed in town by boat, he had a pack on his back filled with specimens of plants. He said to one of the workers on the wharf:

"Where can I find Mr. Audubon of this town?"

"There he is, yonder," said the worker, pointing to Audubon who was standing near by and wondering who this "odd fish" might be.

Rafinesque then introduced himself to Audubon as a fellow-naturalist and was made heartily welcome at the Audubon fire-side. The amiable but strange visitor stayed three weeks at the home of his new friend. During this time he made many excursions with Audubon, collected many species of plants, birds, and fish, and enjoyed himself hugely.

Host and guest were alike in many ways. Both were energetic, enthusiastic, and impractical! Audubon was primarily an artist and Rafinesque a scientist, but their interests met in the common field of natural history.

During his first night with the Audubons, Rafinesque created an uproar in the course of which he wrecked the violin Audubon always kept with him. Everybody had gone to bed and all was quiet when suddenly there were shouts heard from Rafinesque's room and the sound of repeated whacks and running feet. Audubon dashed to investigate. By candlelight he viewed a strange scene.

"There he was in his nightshirt," said

Audubon, "running about the room and smashing at flying bats with my violin, which was already a wreck when I arrived. He wanted to collect the bats because he said they were a new species."

Poor Audubon! The violin was a Cremona, a valuable instrument. But he good-naturedly helped Rafinesque collect a few of the bats that had flown in through an open window. They had been attracted by insects fluttering around the lighted candle in the visitor's bedroom. Worse than the destruction of the violin was another thing that happened during Rafinesque's stay in Henderson, but in this affair it was Audubon who did the damage.

You must remember that horse play and practical joking of all kinds were common in those early rough-and-ready days along the Ohio. Audubon was fond of fun and he had an easy victim in the believing Rafines-

Violin in hand, he was smashing at flying bats.

que. Because the lively visitor almost turned cartwheels of joy over every new species he came upon and wrote down all the information his host gave him on such species, Audubon took playful advantage of him. He "invented" ten imaginary fish of the Ohio and Mississippi, giving Rafinesque scientific descriptions, exact measurements, and specific names of the nonexistent fish.

Rafinesque, a few years later, published a book on the fish of the Ohio River and its tributaries, and included in it Audubon's ten imaginary species!

Audubon lived to regret this bit of foolery and he regretted it for two reasons. First, he was really fond of Rafinesque and was sorry he had put him in the position of publishing nonsense in a supposedly scientific book. Second, the imaginary fish came to life again when some of Audubon's paintings, sketches, and notes on birdlife were challenged as inaccurate or imaginary. His critics said that if Audubon could invent fish, he might invent other things, too. All this, however, came up years later.

When Rafinesque departed from Henderson some three weeks after his arrival, Audubon was left with a problem that was getting worse day by day. This was the mill, the "infernal mill" that was grinding him down.

17

"The Mercantile business did not suit me"

TIMES were hard all along the Ohio. Forty banks failed in a matter of months, including the Bank of Henderson that still owed money to Audubon and Bakewell for lumber that was used in the bank building. The region was flooded with worthless paper money that had been issued by the banks that failed.

"I've had enough," said Tom Bakewell to Audubon. "You take over my share of the mill."

Audubon did, though it was merely adding to his burden. He bought a tract of forest and hired woodchoppers to fell trees to provide logs for the sawmill. The woodchoppers took his money and disappeared down river without ever cutting down a single tree. Audubon was swept under by this flood of misfortunes. The mill was seized by creditors. Audubon owed more than he could pay and he was sent to jail in Louisville for debt. This time he had really hit bottom. When he was turned loose as an acknowledged bankrupt, he had nothing but his gun, his sketches, and the clothes on his back. This was in 1819.

It was the low point in his life in a business way, and it was also the turning point that set his feet on the road to fame. He had met final and complete failure as a "businessman." He would keep no more stores or shops of any kind. He would build no more mills! He was not fitted for life as a merchant or tradesman.

But he could sketch and paint birds better than anybody else in the country! He would now cut himself clear of everything else and devote all his time and efforts to completing a series of water-color paintings, life-size, of all the birds of North America. Never after he was jailed for debt in Louisville did he engage in any business venture except the activities that had to do with publishing and selling his works as an artist and naturalist. At this business, strange to say, he was to become an outstanding success.

But not immediately! Far from it. When he walked away from the Louisville jail he had no money with which to house and feed his family. Then it was that Lucy Audubon took charge.

"I'll look after myself and the boys," said Lucy. "You keep at your sketching and painting of birds until the work is done as you always planned it."

And that is how it was for the next six years, from 1820 to 1826. Mrs. Audubon became a governess and school teacher. She

The innkeeper posed for a portrait by Audubon.

made enough money to support herself and the youngsters and even had a little extra to help out her wandering husband from time to time.

He really was a wandering husband. He traveled down the Ohio and Mississippi rivers to New Orleans and painted the dead birds he found in the markets as well as the live birds he found in the Louisiana bayous. He traveled the roads and rivers back to Louisville. He searched the woods and the swamps for new species of birds. He drew portraits to pay his way. He sketched the captain of a river boat and was paid in gold and he did the portrait of an innkeeper to pay for a night's food and lodging. When Audubon offered to draw the likeness of anyone, the usual query was:

"How much?"

The answer varied according to the wealth or position of the person being sketched.

The price might be anything from a good meal to five dollars or more. This went on for three years. During nearly two of those years Audubon had with him a half-grown boy by the name of Joseph Mason who was his pupil as well as his companion. The youngster had genuine talent. Under the instruction of his teacher, he soon reached the point where he was allowed to paint branches, tree trunks, shrubs, leaves, and flowers that serve as background for the birds in some of Audubon's famous paintings.

Audubon gave lessons to other pupils, too, when he could find them. In New Orleans he gathered so many pupils for art lessons that he was confident he could support his family by this means. He lured Lucy, against her better judgment, into giving up a teaching position in Cincinnati to join him in New Orleans, bringing the children with her.

But Audubon's art pupils soon drifted away, and once more it was up to Lucy to support herself and the children. She soon found a teaching position with a family in Feliciana Parish, Louisiana, and eventually opened a private school there that did well. Indeed, it provided support for Lucy and the children for five years.

On April 5, 1824, Audubon arrived in Philadelphia. He had progressed so far with his sketches and paintings of North American birds that he decided it was time to find a publisher for his great work. And subscribers, or buyers, for it, too! He considered Philadelphia the center of culture of the United States, though possibly the citizens of Boston and New York would not have agreed with him. Certainly in Philadelphia there were artists and scientists and doctors and teachers . . . and rich merchants. There were also old acquaintances who remembered Audubon from his younger days at Mill Grove.

He met the famous artists, Thomas Sully and Rembrandt Peale. He met other naturalists. And he was allowed to display his drawings and paintings at the Academy of Natural Sciences where they were highly praised by some viewers and severely criticized by others.

Alexander Wilson, who had been dead more than ten years by this time, had published his *American Ornithology* in Philadelphia. There were some who thought Wilson's work was superior to the drawings and paintings now put forward by Audubon. In this group was George Ord, a good ornithologist who helped Wilson, edited the last volume of the *American Ornithology* after Wilson's death, and wrote his biography. Among other things, Ord said that rattlesnakes do not climb bushes or trees . . . and

Audubon had a painting showing a rattlesnake being attacked by a pair of mocking-
birds at their nest in a bush or low tree. In
other words, Ord hinted that Audubon was
a "nature faker."

This led to a hubbub. Some joined Ord in
the attack. Others supported Audubon and
offered evidence to show that rattlesnakes
do, at times, climb bushes or low trees.
Eventually the rattlesnake debate was decided in favor of Audubon, but perhaps some
other criticisms by Ord were justified.

Charles Bonaparte, wealthy young ornithologist and a nephew of Napoleon Bonaparte, admired Audubon's work and wanted
to buy some of his drawings. Young Bonaparte planned to have them engraved by a
man named Lawson, a fine workman and a
native of Scotland. However, Lawson, who
was a stout supporter of Wilson's work, de-

nounced Audubon's drawings and paintings as no good at all.

"You may buy them if you please," he said to Charles Bonaparte, "but I'll not engrave them. They're not worth it."

Audubon packed up, left Philadelphia, and sadly resumed his wanderings. He went to New York, to Buffalo, and to Pittsburgh, living from hand to mouth and paying his way as best he could by sketching men, women, and children. He met strange adventures, and everywhere and always added to his knowledge of natural history and his collection of bird paintings. One important thing had come of his visit to Philadelphia. An admirer of his paintings had said to him:

"You must publish your work in Europe. You will find the best engravers there."

The more he traveled in this country, the

more Audubon became convinced that his Philadelphia friend was right. He would have to go to Europe to get his work published. But to do that would take money, a good deal of money! Where or how could he lay hands on such a sum?

Early in 1825 he rejoined his family in Louisiana and became a teacher, like Lucy. He taught painting. He taught dancing. He taught French. He gave violin lessons. He had sixty pupils in one class! He made money, more than he had ever made before in his life. At the end of 1825, due largely to Lucy's earnings, he had enough to pay his way abroad. The Audubons now had everything at stake.

"To England!" said Lucy, as she kissed him good-bye.

"To England!" echoed her husband.

This, they fervently hoped, would be the turning point of their lives.

18

"I continued to draw birds and quadrupeds"

*I*T IS difficult for people of the twentieth century to picture the long voyage of sixty-five days that Audubon took just in order to get to England. With the air travel of to-day making the trip only an overnight hop, we cannot help wondering how a person would spend the long weeks of an ocean crossing in the year 1826.

But when the passenger was Audubon we need to wonder no more. For we can picture him sitting out on a wind-lashed deck, wrapped in blankets, perhaps, his little sketchbook in his lap.

There is no such thing as an idle moment for a man with such a fiery aim in life. Every second of the day brought him just

He watched the sea birds dart through the spray.

that much closer to the realization of his life's dream.

He had pencils and paper. He had his own field notes. And he had that great desire to *keep drawing.* So, while other passengers might have gossiped and complained of the heavy seas and waited impatiently for the cry of "Land ho," Audubon was happily occupied. If he grew tired of sketching, he could watch for sea birds.

One morning he might finish the first rough sketch he had made of some bird still

to be painted. He had an uncanny memory
for the kind of day on which he had made
the original sketch. So, now, referring to
his notes on the bird's shading and size, he
could recapture the feeling of life that made
his bird drawings different from any that
had ever been done.

Someone once said he took the wires out
of birds. In other words, he did not copy the
method of the other naturalists, which was
simply to draw a stuffed bird. No, he put
them in true-to-life poses, as a glance at his
goshawk, ruby-throated hummingbird, blue-
winged teal, and snowy owl will show.

They are exciting paintings, full of the
feeling of a gray day or of a fine one. Composition—the way the parts of a picture are
put together—was becoming more and more
of a challenge to him. It was not enough
to paint an accurate likeness . . . the design
must be pleasing, too.

So, he sketched many black-and-white arrangements on his journey toward England.

He must have often put his sketchbook down, though, and thought of good Lucy, now so far away. When would he see her? And would he be proud to tell her of his success?

Would he be successful?

He stopped this doubting daydreaming and began to draw feverishly again. His Journal tells us, too, of all the birds he observed on this crossing.

To give an idea of the thoroughness with which Audubon examined a bird, study the notes he made in his Journal on the brown pelican:

"Length 4 feet, 2½ inches from the tip of the Bill to the end of the Toes . . . the eye is brown, pretty large and situated in the skin that so covers the cheeks and jaws of the bill . . . the upper of the head and side of the neck running along the pouch of a mole color. The hind head ornamented with a crest of slender feathers of 1½ inch in length . . . the upper plumage of the neck, assuming a silky appearance and much worn by resting on the back and shoulders of the Bird.

"Shoulders and back covered with pointed, small feathers, the former light ash in their centers . . . some edged with brown. . . . The tail rounded, extended measured 7½ feet the second joint 9 inches closing on the body reaching to the beginning of the neck and when closed the tips reach the end of the tail, the first 9 primary quills white to their points below and about ½ above; the feathering dark brownish black cast.

"Secondaries much the same . . . tertials broad falling over the back part of the body to the root of the tail; feathers of the shoulders of a light ash, some edged with brown,

others with black, quills very slender and
black . . . whole under part white and in
some specimen silvery. Legs strong and
muscular far behind. 4 toes webbed in
connection . . . the whole of a bluish green-
ish yellow. Claws blunt, much hooked the
longest pectinated inwardly . . . the bird
emitting a strong disagreeable fish smell.
Weighed 6½ pounds.

"On dissection it was a male, the stom-
ach very long and slender, fleshy contain-
ing only about 50 slender blue worms all
alive about 2½ inches long . . . the gut
measured 10 feet about the size of a mod-
erate swan's quill. The bird was killed on
Lake Barataria by Mr. Hunter Gilbert.
The rump and the root of the tail was covered with a thin coating of oily fat extremely rancid, and much air was contained
between the whole of the skin and flesh of
the body; the bones of the wings and legs

although extremely hard and difficult to break were very thin and light and perfectly empty."

What an impressive array of notes to make about just one bird!

And Audubon had hundreds of such notes.

No wonder the time did not hang heavily on his voyage to England!

No wonder he seized every day as an opportunity to study more of his notes, to make rough sketches of the birds he had yet to paint, and to write in his Journal.

For his plan, remember, was to sell his series before he had even finished drawing and painting all the birds to be included in it. He would show what he had finished, take orders, and then draw the other birds while he continued to sign new subscribers.

But suppose he could get no new subscribers!

As the boat neared England he refused to let such a gloomy thought take hold of him.

He might have looked over his portfolio with some care and taken out the letters of introduction which had been given to him by friends in Philadelphia and in New Orleans.

Though people have called Audubon a moody man at times, his disposition was the sort that would not allow him to remain long in any depressed state of mind. Even though he was lonely and even though he must have had doubts about his future, he had a certain basic buoyancy that came to the surface when he needed it most.

And it came now, as he moved down the gangplank and put his foot on English soil at Liverpool on July 21, 1826.

19

"I am well received everywhere"

HE WAS an odd-looking fellow to be sure
when he strode down the main street of
Liverpool that early morning in 1826.

Always slim and agile—those long walks
through the woods took care of that—he
cut a dashing figure. He wore his clothes
with a careless grace and his long hair fell
in ringlets to his shoulders.

People turned around on the street and
stared at him. Was he an American? A
Frenchman? His speech was a mixture of
both.

That he was an artist was certain. The
huge portfolio showed it. But one writer
had this to say about his appearance:

"Brave is the exhibition of flowing locks;
they flow over the ears and over the coat-

collars; you can smell the bear's grease across the street."

Audubon took all these comments in stride. He was smart enough to know that anything that made people turn around and stare was just so much the better for his work. He wanted to be talked about. He wanted to be entertained by influential people.

The drawing rooms of fashionable homes in Liverpool were, at the time of Audubon's arrival, like fashionable drawing rooms anywhere, at any time. In other words, the people who met in them were always anxious to have something different to talk about. Something new. Something educational or, if not educational, at least entertaining.

The appearance of a fine-figured Frenchman with long hair flowing over his shoulders would have been enough to attract their attention in itself. But when, after pointing him out, it was said that he was a brilliant artist and a naturalist as well, the fashionable homes hummed with gossip. Maybe the visitor would come to dinner!

There was one Liverpool family to whom Audubon carried a letter of introduction—the Rathbones. They were so kind that he was forever indebted to them for their hospitality. For their part, they were honestly impressed by him and felt that he had something of benefit to their host of wealthy friends.

So they made sure that he was introduced to everyone they knew who was interested in natural history and in painting.

Audubon seems to have lived in a sort of dream world for a few days after he arrived in England. At first he was a little dazzled by all the attention he received. Then he began to weigh the flattery for what it was worth and saw that it was worth very little if it did not result in subscriptions to his *Birds of America*.

Stories of the artist buzzed around the tea table.

Still, he had occasion to write enthusiastic letters to Lucy. For one thing, just about a week after his arrival he was invited to exhibit his work at the Royal Institution in Liverpool. This was a feat of a sort, since he was practically a stranger.

And it was just the beginning of a series of invitations that ran from formal dinners to teas, with a few sittings for portraits fitted in between times. Though Audubon was a man of splendid health and often worked fourteen hours without stopping, the pace of socializing, plus all his painting, was almost more than he could endure.

He wrote: "I go to dine, at six, seven or eight o'clock in the evening, and it is often one or two when the party breaks up; then painting all day, with my correspondence which increases daily, makes my head feel like an immense hornet's nest, and my body wearied beyond all calculation; yet it has to be done; those who have my best interests at heart tell me I must *not refuse* a single invitation."

Probably he would never have been able to keep up the pace except for the fact that he never ate or drank too much.

One of his most pleasant meetings was with the great British writer, Sir Walter Scott. Naturally Audubon was a little timid about being introduced to such a celebrity, but he had no reason to be. Scott's admiration for him was most warm.

The two had several enjoyable talks on such subjects as painting and natural history. The letters that the great writer gave to Audubon he prized very highly indeed.

But he was impatient for buyers now. He must get subscribers.

"I will publish this Great Work myself," he said. Just repeating the words aloud filled him with a thrill such as he had never before experienced.

Surely now, as he saw the realization of his dreams coming closer every day, he must have enjoyed looking back over the years. Perhaps the memory of the people who had laughed at him was fading a little now. The physical hardships he had undergone in pursuit of specimens . . . they were nothing. The good things, the strong things, were his own zeal, his own self-confidence, and the knowledge that Lucy was always with him. Even though she was now many miles away on the other shore of the Atlantic, she was in his mind daily. He must have felt her encouragement just as if they were sitting at home and she were asking him about the way he drew a certain bird in flight.

But as so often happened in Audubon's life, a blow fell just when things seemed to be sailing along merrily. The man in Scotland to whom he had entrusted the engraving of his drawings ran into difficulty in his shop, and Audubon was left with the problem of finding another engraver.

Though he had met with some success in Scotland as far as attracting attention to his work, and indeed, as far as getting subscribers was concerned, he felt he should now move on to London. Here he met the man who did more for his *Birds of America* than anyone else. He was Havell, the well-known engraver.

20

"The engravings are thought beautiful"

ROBERT HAVELL, senior, was a man of some reputation in London at the time Audubon became acquainted with him. He was very much interested in the beautiful life-size drawings of birds that now lay before him. At the same time, he realized that the great task of reproducing them would take years . . . more years than he perhaps would live to see. So he recommended another engraver, one whose work he had noticed. By a strange chance he did not know that the man whose unsigned work he had approved was his own son.

Audubon was disappointed to learn that the older man would not take on the assignment, but he agreed to try out the son. To test the young engraver's work, Audubon asked that a copy be made of his Prothonotary Warbler, that dazzling little orange-yellow bird.

The result delighted him. He was excited to find an engraver who could copy every fine line, every delicate gradation of color, with such infinite care.

Thus the partnership of Havell & Son and their relationship to Audubon was begun.

And now it looked as if the last hard uphill road were before him. If he kept on working to get more subscribers, a triumphant moment was in sight.

As you read of his European experiences, you must be wondering what kind of man he was to leave Lucy and his two boys for such a long time. A year had passed and he had not seen them. That would be unheard of in a family today, but in those days you must remember that some men's occupations demanded long absences.

A whaling captain, for example, might sail for years before coming into his home port. Then, at last, he would lift that long spyglass and see his wife anxiously waiting at the very top of their house on a little promenade called the "widow's walk."

When she knew it was about time for him to be coming home, she would spend many hours on this perch, watching the horizon for the first sign of a sail. She might even have a long spyglass herself.

These whaling captains left their home ports prepared for that long separation.

But Audubon, in his usual impulsive way, had done no such planning. When he had been gone for well over a year, he wrote to Lucy that it was his intention to remain in England as long as he had drawings to keep his work going . . . say for five years. As soon as he was really settled, he would write for her to join him there.

"When that does take place, I will have everything ready to receive my Sweet Wife in Comfort."

Though there are no letters from Lucy which show her state of mind, we can read between the lines of *his* and imagine that she must have been a little stern.

Perhaps like any good wife she wrote:

"Yes, my dear, I am delighted that things seem to be progressing so well. I would never lose faith in you; you know that. But I would like to see an itemized accounting of the state of your business some day. It does not seem wise for me to leave America until I can be sure that we will not go into debt as, alas, we have done so often before."

Poor Lucy, hundreds of miles away, teaching school to support herself and wondering if her gay, lovable husband would ever amount to anything!

We can tell that she *might* have written

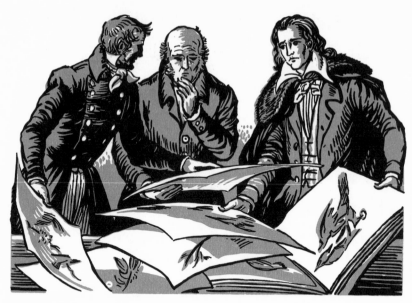

Everywhere he sought subscribers to his bird prints.

a letter like that because there is one from
Audubon dated August 25th, 1827, in which
he briskly summed up the situation as he
wrote to his son Victor.

"I have rather more than one hundred
subscribers. I issue 5 series or numbers of
my work per annum which amount to
rather more at present than 1000 guineas.
. . . This sum I conceive quite sufficient in
itself to enable me to have your Mama and
John with me to live in comfort, and as

soon as I have 100 more subscribers I will write to you also to come if it be agreeable to your wishes with a view to settle you in a good Commercial House in Liverpool."

It is an indication of Audubon's gentle nature that he was interested in having his son come to England only "if it be agreeable to your (the son's) wishes." Perhaps he was remembering the lack of understanding his own father had shown when he himself wanted to paint as a boy.

Then in other letters to Lucy he protested his love and said it would mean much to him to see her again but that "Prudence" restrained him from sending for her just then.

"I rely much on my industry, activity, and sobriety and so pray for me and I think I will bring it to a good bearing," he wrote.

Victory was in sight, but there would still be years of tiring and often disappointing work.

21

"Thy husband can not bear to be outdone"

"The king has subscribed!"

This was the exciting news that went from Audubon to engraver and from engraver to tradesmen and then to all the countryside. Yes, George the Fourth was the dazzling name added to his subscription list. The Duchess of Clarence was another.

By this time Audubon's pictures had attracted the attention of all the leading scientists of the day. He, an unknown American, had shown some of them at the Royal Institution of Edinburgh. Later, he exhibited his work in London at the Linnaean and Royal Societies, both of which elected him to fellowships.

Some of his letters to Lucy reporting these honors were boyish in their enthusiasm, but as the months went by there was also an undercurrent of shrewdness and good old-fashioned common sense. He was impressed by all the entertaining done for him but he realized, and mentioned more than once, that this amounted to nothing if it did not result in more subscribers for "My Great Work."

He believed so strongly, so fiercely in himself that gradually he was making other people believe in him, too.

Self-confidence is one lesson to be learned from Audubon. Perseverance, under all kinds of difficulties, is another.

He *would* not be discouraged. He would work sixteen hours a day and fall into bed exhausted. But early the next morning he would be at work again with the soaring hope that morning always brought to him.

He would make *everyone* love his *Birds of America.*

We can picture him now, unrested after only a few hours' sleep, packing his drawings in that huge portfolio and hailing a stagecoach for another selling tour. A portrait of him painted at about this time shows him in a green coat, with a fur-edged crimson cloak thrown over his arm.

Scotland and England were not the only places in which he engaged in the role of traveling salesman. He visited Paris, too, where he met with fair success. Whenever we think of the trips he took we must compare them with travel conditions today. If we keep this in mind it gives us a much truer idea of what he accomplished. By slow boat, by stagecoach, in cold and in rain he pressed on.

He must have had many lonely days and nights.

He must have longed not only for a sight of his wife and boys, but also for a glimpse of his beloved American woods.

The delight of a leisurely bird walk in Louisiana had been denied him now for almost two years. The refreshment that he always felt after a canter through the Pennsylvania countryside was something he could dream about as a luxury he had enjoyed long ago when he had managed his father's farm at Mill Grove.

Now, in less than two years, he had changed from a happy-go-lucky sketcher of birds to a grim and realistic businessman.

Oh, he was painting and polishing, too, but his day-to-day task was principally selling.

Finally, when he felt that his association

with Havell, his engraver, was on a sound
enough basis, he made plans to go back to
America and prevail on Lucy to return to
England with him.

He felt that his work was in good hands,
since Mr. John Children, a member of the
British Museum staff, was to take charge of
things.

The Havells would still do the engraving,
but Mr. Children would supervise the dis-
tribution of the prints. Audubon sailed
from Portsmouth on April 1, 1829, and arrived in New York just a month later.

He was back in America for the third
time in his life, but this time he was a person of some importance. The aristocracy
of France, Scotland, and England had vied
with one another to have him accept their
dinner invitations. He was a celebrity at
last!

Even this joyful arrival in New York did
not give him the idea of spending a holiday. To Audubon, there was no such thing
as a vacation. Not even a half holiday!
He stayed in New York only long enough
to exhibit his drawings at the Lyceum of
Natural History. Then he went on to
Great Egg Harbor in New Jersey where he
planned to observe and draw water birds.

He did not rush to the arms of his beloved Lucy?

No. He was still the man of genius and
he must make every second count so far as
getting new bird material was concerned.

Naturally this delay did not please his
wife.

There was an exchange of letters, with
his son Victor as the go-between in some.
Even then, Audubon was stubborn enough
to go on with his plans for painting more
American birds while he had the chance.

Listen to his report of that stay in America:

"I am at work," he wrote in October, 1829, "and have done much but I wish I had eight pairs of hands, and another body to shoot the specimens. . . . Forty-two drawings in four months comprising ninety-five birds from Eagles downwards, with plants, nests, flowers and sixty kinds of eggs."

During this time the letters that he and Lucy exchanged were bringing them closer together at least in *plans* for a reunion.

He started a leisurely journey down the Ohio, stopped to see his sons (now taller than he) at Louisville, and at last met Lucy in Feliciana Parish in Louisiana.

What a reunion it must have been! The clock was turned back while they repeated their old life. He roamed the woods, hunting and drawing as he had done in the early days of their marriage. She encouraged him with more hope than ever, now that she could see him and hear him tell of his success in England. She was getting ready to go back with him, too.

They might have stayed on happily in Feliciana except for a disturbing note from Havell, Audubon's London engraver. *Subscriptions were falling off: the sooner Audubon returned to England the better.*

The Audubons made arrangements to do this immediately. On their way north, they stopped in Washington where President Andrew Jackson received them. Picture Lucy, the quiet governess-wife, a-flutter as she is presented to the President. Her husband must have made little of her excitement, because meeting distinguished citizens was a familiar experience to him by this time.

"They are only people like ourselves, my dear," he must have told her gravely. "We should judge them by their characters and not by their positions."

After he had done several more paintings, they sailed from New York to England on April 1, 1830, heavily burdened by shells and insects and furs and bird skins that he had promised his friends on the other side. He hoped to sell some, too.

22

"I am . . . dull, too mournful"

BACK IN ENGLAND again, he regained some of his subscribers and picked up the task of selling his "Great Work," just as if he had never been interrupted by that trip to America.

Lucy, who must have left her position as governess with some sadness and uncertainty, could see, when she had been in London only a few days, that he had been in great need of her. All details connected with his tremendous project now fell on her shoulders. She answered his letters, arranged his appointments, took care of his clothes (for he was paying more attention to dress) and, most important, was near him at the end of the day to listen to his problems. That was her sweet burden.

Lucy was always there to encourage him.

For a while his spirits soared under this new arrangement.

And then, once again, just when there seemed to be a good reason for feeling hopeful, something happened to plunge him into despair. This time it was a series of complaints from subscribers who were not satisfied with the quality of several of the engravings.

Audubon had to admit that they were right. He wrote a sad note to Havell in which he said that "your engraver must be dismissed or become considerably more careful." He added that if he should find the same complaints as he went from one town to another he would abandon the publication of his work and return "to my own woods until I leave this World for a better one."

How utterly discouraged he must have been to say: "I would rather live in Peace in the woods than be tormented here when I do all in my power to Please."

Poor Audubon! This was one of his lowest moments.

If Lucy had not been there to encourage him he might have decided to forget the whole Great Work and carry out his threat to go back to the woods.

But she knew that the situation was not

hopeless. She knew that Havell would see to it that his engravers and colorers lived up to their first fine work.

As indeed they did! The quality of their work improved so much that the subscribers who had canceled decided to renew.

Audubon was working now on what he called an "Ornithological Biography," a life history of all the birds he had painted.

In order to be sure of his scientific facts he visited libraries and bookstores with pencil and paper, making notes on the Latin as well as the English spelling. Remember that French was his native tongue and that writing in English was a troublesome task for him.

But he kept at it as he kept at everything else.

By this time he and Lucy had moved to Edinburgh for a season. There, Audubon was helped greatly by a young naturalist named William MacGillivray, after whom Audubon later named a warbler. The two men worked on the "Ornithological Biography," with quiet Lucy copying the manuscript and making many corrections in grammar, no doubt.

It is amusing to read in Audubon's journal about this time that they took a trip when they "traveled by that extraordinary road called the railway, at the rate of 24 miles an hour."

It must have seemed that they were whizzing through the English countryside.

Some time after this Audubon did a little figuring on paper. He said to himself, and readers of this day must surely agree, that it was truly remarkable that $40,000 should have passed through his hands in connection with the *Birds of America*.

Things were moving along so satisfactorily now that he longed to return to Amer-

ica and explore Florida. He knew he would
find birds there which he had never seen,
and he wanted his series to be complete.
Only then would it be a life-size record of
every native bird!

So he and Lucy sailed for America on
August 2, 1831.

23

"My Work suffers for the want of greater patronage"

"LISTEN to the sea gulls screaming," said Lucy as she and her husband boarded the vessel for home. Big gray and white birds circled the ship, swooped down and up again, their shrill cries mingling with the shouts of the deck hands.

The Audubons settled themselves quickly and then strolled about, Lucy a little sad, no doubt, to see the shore of England growing dim. She had enjoyed a busy but pleasant time there, visiting old friends and relatives, in addition to all her work with her husband. Now, dressed perhaps in a long gray cloak and little gray bonnet, she put her arm through his and watched his

eagle-bright eyes as he followed the swooping and darting of the birds.

The trip passed without incident.

As soon as they were on American soil
she returned once more to Louisville to
teach.

But her husband had that other aim—
that Florida exploration.

Today you think of Florida as a sunshine
vacation land with luxury hotels and a
huge citrus industry. In the days of Audubon it was a wilderness. Indians—the
Seminoles—lived there, and only a brave
man, one who would not shudder at the
sight of a long-mouthed alligator, would
dare to penetrate the swamps.

Audubon was in Florida during November and, though some extremes of tempera-
ture were reported, he wrote that they had
actually had very few cold nights. The
trees were green. Butterflies brightened

the air and many flowers were in bloom.

As Audubon's letters and journals show, he was not a man who complained easily. However, he said of this Florida trip that he doubted if ever a man had undergone more fatigue. He had scrambled through the "fan Palmettoes" and long grass and waded through mud—always in search of some new species of bird.

Much of his time was spent in collecting shells, too, and insects and birds' eggs. Nothing to do with nature was too tiny to escape his eye.

He was not very much impressed with Florida, however. He called it wild and dreary, and he was made so uneasy by the hundreds of alligators that he did not dare let his good Newfoundland dog go in the river.

Reports of all these experiences were made in his regular letters to Lucy, whom he always addressed as "My dearest Friend." He told her, too, of his meeting with the "Reverend Mr. Bachman," a resident of Charleston, South Carolina, who also had a great interest in natural history and would not hear of Audubon's staying at a hotel.

"My house is yours," was what he said to Audubon in effect.

From that moment on, Mr. Bachman proved to be one of Audubon's closest friends. (Incidentally, it was he who gave him the Newfoundland dog.)

That invitation to stay at his home was too tempting to resist. The Bachman home was large enough to provide Audubon with three rooms—one room to skin the birds, another room for drawing, and another for sleeping. Audubon considered it such a stroke of luck to run into a kindred spirit of this sort that his letters to Lucy for a few days were full of his old-time enthusiasm

The blue heron, curlews and sandpipers delighted him.

If only she and his two sons were with him, he said, his happiness would be complete.

But it was only at night, while he was writing to her, that he allowed himself such pleasant "castles in Spain." During the day it was the same old story. Shooting, skinning, drawing.

By December 5th he had portrayed 17 different species, had collected hundreds of shells, and about 100 bird skins. His great-

est joy lay in finding a new species of
vulture.

Lucy, settling down to her old teaching
routine, must have been quietly proud that
she was no longer Mrs. Audubon, wife of
that scatterbrained bird fancier, but Mrs.
John James Audubon, wife of the *famous
naturalist*. The news of her husband's success in England had spread to this country,
so now she could indeed hold her head high
as she walked down the street.

Audubon, meanwhile, was not resting on
his laurels.

Ignoring the discomforts of Florida, brush-
ing aside the sand fleas and mosquitoes, he
went doggedly about the business at hand.
The blue heron and white ibis delighted
him. And so did the curlews and the sandpipers and the cranes.

He left Florida, tanned and in high spirits, after four months.

"I will go to Washington," he said, "and see if I can not prevail on the government to finance an expedition to the Rockies."

This had always been a pet ambition way back in his mind.

But here he met with disappointment. He was told that the project would be too expensive.

Did he decide to take a little vacation now that his great work was proceeding well?

Not Audubon!

He immediately made plans to go north— to explore the coast of Labrador and find, perhaps, the nesting places of gannets, razor-billed auks, guillemots, and those "sea parrots" of almost incredible appearance, the puffins.

Meanwhile Lucy was attending to some important correspondence.

24

"Keep up a good correspondence with England"

(*letter to Lucy*)

*T*HERE IS perhaps no better way of judging a person than by his or her letters, especially if they were sent with no thought of their being published.

Lucy Audubon, about whom so little has been written, has revealed herself thus far through her husband only. We see her first as a wealthy girl who, because she fell in love, married an impractical artist.

Then through the years, as Audubon grows in personality, she begins to take on a more positive shape in our minds. What patience! What faithfulness!

Among the few echoes we have of Lucy, there is a letter written to Mr. Havell when Audubon was out of touch with mail from

England. Picture her, after a day of teaching, penning this letter seriously, almost sternly by candlelight. Read it thoughtfully. Through it you meet Lucy.

Louisville, March 22, 1832

To ROBT HAVELL, *Esq.*
77 Oxford Street, London

My dear Sir,
    Your favor of Jan. 31 has this moment been handed to me . . . and now to refer to your letter I am very sorry any expressions of mine have offended you . . . that was not our intention, but whatever remarks I made were in consequence of the facts which I stated to you respecting the plates and work, and from authority of my husband repeated in his letter since we parted, to give you notice of any errors that you who are always at the work can not see so clearly as those who only occasionally look it over, and I assure you Mr. Audubon will thank me for pointing out to you those things which I have and on which his success and reputation so much depend.
    Mr. A. and I are of one mind, we do not doubt your Zeal nor good intentions, but we think ourselves at liberty to state any changes we think for our benefit and

My son and myself now act for Mr.
Audubon, . . . I did not write in anger to
you but in sorrow in consequence of the
complaints from Philadelphia. . . . We
have the utmost confidence in your in-
tentions but we think it possible you may
require advice, and hoping you now understand my motives as most friendly to-
wards you I will dismiss the subject. . . .

Mr. A. was on the 17th of February in
the centre of Florida suffering from dep-
rivation of every sort. I must now con-
clude with every good wish for your
health and prosperity and hope to find
both you and Mrs. Havell well.

Sincerely yours,

L. AUDUBON

Her directness is something to admire
here and so is her common sense. She did
not write pages and pages of complaints
about the quality of his engravings which
had been criticized in this country. She
simply stated her case, clearly and firmly,
and ended her letter like the gentlewoman
she was. No wonder many people say: "What
would Audubon have been without Lucy?"

25

"All ashore in search of birds, plants, shells"

As WE KNOW, Audubon spent four months or so in Florida, exploring the Everglades and cruising along sunlit keys. He found wonderful birds to collect and paint, but there were few subscribers to be found there. He needed subscribers as well as new species of birds to complete his series. As the printing of the plates continued, he had to get money to meet the bills of Havell in London.

So farewell to Florida! He moved northward where subscribers—or, at least, prospective subscribers—were more abundant.

In May, 1832, he was again in Charleston with his firm friend, the Reverend John Bachman. In June, he was in Philadelphia. He hurried through New York because of much sickness in that city and reached Boston in early summer. He made many good friends who were helpful to him while he was adding new birds and new subscribers to his lists. Most of the summer he spent at Eastport, Maine. What he wanted to do was to go to Labrador, but it was too late in the season to plan on any such trip in 1832.

Now he had to make a decision. Robert Havell was doing as well as he could with the printing in London, but the shipping of the prints to the subscribers and the keeping of accounts was a heavy burden to the engraver. So he wrote letters begging Audubon to return to London.

However, Audubon had work to do in this country. There were more species to be added to his bird paintings. He felt, too, that he could get many added subscribers to his work if he remained in the United States for another year.

What he did was to send his son Victor to London in his place. Victor sailed in October. The other members of the Audubon family spent the winter in Boston. You must remember that Victor was only twenty-three years old when he was sent to London to handle his father's affairs. It was a big responsibility for such a young man. Victor wasn't sure that he was up to it.

"I have great faith in you, my son!" said Audubon.

And that faith was completely justified. If you read the letters of Audubon you will see how lucky he was to have such a wife as Lucy and to have two such sons as Victor and John—and how well he knew it.

Now that Victor was in London, Audubon could make ready for his trip to Labrador in 1833. In January of that year he received a golden eagle that had been caught in the White Mountains of New Hampshire in a trap set for a fox. He spent fourteen days painting the golden eagle and worked so hard at it that he had a "seizure," probably a heart attack. However, he was soon well again and hard at work painting more pictures and finding new subscribers for his great project.

In May he was in Eastport, Maine, with his son John and four young men who had volunteered to go along as helpers on the trip to Labrador. Audubon had chartered the schooner *Ripley*, crew and all, for the summer. It was a fairly new vessel of 106 tons. On June 9th the wind at last was favorable and they set sail for the famous "bird islands" of the Gulf of St. Lawrence and the rocky coasts of Newfoundland and Labrador. These were the nesting grounds of gannets, razor-billed auks, murres, guillemots, puffins, dovekies, kittiwakes, blackbacked gulls, and other such birds of the sea.

Sometimes a dark rocky mass rising out of the water might seem snow-covered as the *Ripley* sailed toward it. Then, when the voyagers drew near, the "snow" rose in thousands of whirling white flakes that were gulls or gannets in frightened flight above their eggs or nestlings.

"Why are they disturbed so much?" asked young John Audubon.

"They take us for eggers," said one of the crew. He meant that professional egg-hunters had so often raided the nesting grounds in this region that the birds took flight as soon as any ship drew near them.

The Audubon group took only the few eggs and birds they needed for scientific purposes. Yet the damage that man and his ways can do to birds is shown by the fact that three species that flourished in Audubon's day are now extinct. One is the Carolina paroquet found throughout much of the South a century ago. Another is the passenger pigeon whose vast flocks, as old stories have it, "darkened the sky" while they flew along. The third is the Labrador duck that Audubon found on the coast of Labrador on this very trip. We still have Audubon's painting of it, but the species is extinct.

Inland from the Labrador coast Audubon and his young helpers found the traveling hard. Insects pestered them, too. But here they discovered nests of the snow bunting and the blackpoll warbler. They found an uncommon sparrow that Audubon named for one of his young helpers on the trip, Tom Lincoln. He called it Lincoln's sparrow and it still bears that name. Where they came

As the ship drew near, swarms of birds arose.

upon scattered patches of spruce, they found the merry little crossbills breeding.

It was a great trip. Summer is short in that northern region, however, and they turned back in August, reaching Eastport on the last day of that month. They had left the ship in Nova Scotia and had gone overland. Now they had to return to Eastport to gather up the material that the *Ripley* carried to its home port, the collections they had made in the field and put in bundles for later study. Included in the collections were eggs, bird skins, nests, mosses, plants, and shells.

By September, Audubon was in New York, gradually going southward to spend the winter at the Bachman homestead in Charleston. On this trip he collected a few more birds and gained five new subscribers. He was hard at work over his drawing board through the winter and had a fine collection of added paintings ready for Havell when, with his wife and younger son, he sailed for England in April, 1834.

Now the Audubons were united in London and for the next two years they worked as a team in pushing forward the great project. The printing had begun in 1826. Ten years later the painter, the engraver and the colorists were still at their labors and the end was not yet in sight.

When you examine an original Audubon print, you realize why the progress was so slow. The amount of detail shown is amazing. Then you must remember that Audubon's plan, which later had to be enlarged, was to publish 200 copies of his work, each of which was to include 400 prints. That meant taking a total of 80,000 impressions from the plates and *putting in the colors on each print by hand!* There were dozens of colorists working in the Havell establish-

ment at one time, with Havell, Audubon, or
one of the Audubon boys watching closely
to see that every last detail of color or tex-
ture was correct.

And always there were changes to be
made as the work progressed. Between the
time the project was started and the date it
was completed, there were financial panics
in England and the United States. Many
original subscribers couldn't keep up their
payments. Some died and their heirs refused to go on with it. New subscribers
were added every year and often a whole
series of prints from the earlier plates had
to be done over again for them.

More important than that, new species of
birds were being found in North America,
and Audubon wanted to have all the known
species of birds of North America depicted
in his great work when it was finished. For

that purpose he returned to the United States in 1836, sailing from Portsmouth on August 2nd and landing in New York on September 8th. Just a year later he was back in England with many new paintings, so many that he had to extend the series to 435 plates instead of the 400 of the original plan.

He had been in Florida, Alabama, Mississippi, and Louisiana. He had visited Texas, then a republic, and had met President Sam Houston in a mud-floored hut in Houston. "Old Hickory," as President Andrew Jackson was called, was Audubon's dinner host in the White House on his way south.

Coming north in 1837, Audubon had shaken the hand of Jackson's successor in the White House, President Van Buren. He had seen and drawn "snipes, gallinules, curlews, night-hawks and herons" on the Gulf Coast. Finally, he had secured specimens of

new birds brought back from the Pacific
Northwest by the Nuttall-Townsend expedition of 1834 and 1835.

At last he was in London to add the final
paintings to his great series and publish them
in triumph, with his wife and boys by his
side. Before another year passed, he had
accomplished it. On June 20, 1838, the
original "elephant edition" of the *Birds of
America*, by J. J. Audubon, was complete in
four great morocco-bound volumes. Many
sets of these books remain in museums, pub-
lic libraries, and private collections as a
monument to the artistry, industry, integrity, and genius of an amazing soul.

26

"I am growing old Fast"

Now we are coming to the end of a story of perseverance that would be hard to equal.

You met the daydreaming young Audubon in France. You saw him grow up and marry. You watched him as he sketched aimlessly in the woods. You followed his failures and shared his feeling of discouragement before he reached that final exciting peak of success. He accomplished the almost impossible task of painting every bird of America, life size, and selling reproductions of those paintings for around $200,000.

Did he have any faults? Of course he did. Do you know anyone who has none? He was impractical, vain perhaps, and certainly hot-tempered when he should have been most patient.

So, like many another famous person, he had enemies. Some questioned his reputation as a naturalist during the famous argument over whether or not a rattlesnake could climb a tree. Others of his enemies believed he owed much, by way of inspiration, to Wilson who also had the idea of painting American birds. And there was Waterton, the British naturalist. He had no love for Audubon.

But these were the exceptions.

Most people who knew him were impressed by his kindness and his unwavering singleness of purpose.

Every so often, in his later journal, a note of wistfulness creeps in. He is not as quick as he was. He tires more easily. He feels that his time is running out and he wants, feverishly, to finish before it is too late.

Portraits of him made about this time

From their porch the Audubons could see the Hudson.

show a middle-aged man with a jaw of almost frightening determination.

What a joy it must have been to him to find out, as he grew older, that his two sons were all that a most ambitious and loving father could ask. Victor was his secretary-

accountant and John was his artist field-
companion. In letters to Victor, Audubon
constantly reminded the young man that
he was very, very proud of him.

And his letters to Lucy are filled with a
mellow kind of joy. "May God Bless and
preserve us and be it His will to grant us
peaceful and Happy old days altogether!"
he wrote to her more than once.

That wish was realized.

His great work was completed in 1838.

He and Lucy bought a house and a little
land on the Hudson River in New York City
and here they lived almost in the fairy-tale
"happy ever after" way. Visitors described
the place as a perfect setting. The Audubons
could sit out on their old-fashioned wooden
porch and see the Hudson stretching north
and south before them. They could hear the
birds and see them in the trees near by.

Though Audubon continued to work here

—he was drawing his *Quadrupeds of America* and planning a smaller edition of the *Birds of America*—his strength gradually left him.

He died, this gentle genius, on January 27, 1851, before he was 67.

He would be astonished today, no doubt, if he could see the way his fame has spread not only through his exciting paintings but through the activities of the Audubon Society which makes his work live on. It labors constantly for the protection of birds as well as for the conservation of all wildlife.

And yet, as we remember his rugged self-confidence, perhaps he would not be surprised at all. Perhaps he would consider it a most fitting and practical monument to his great enthusiasm for the beauties of nature.

Like Saint Francis of Assisi, who too loved creatures, Audubon might point to his magnificent paintings today and say simply: "Here they are then, my little sisters, the birds."

Index

Academy of Natural Sciences, Philadelphia, 111
Accounts, keeping, 162
Alabama, 171
Allegheny Mountains, 68
Alligators, 152–53
America, 47, 64, 150–51
American Ornithology (Wilson), 111
Animals, 17
Atlantic Ocean, 129
Audubon, Captain, 5–6; authority, 11; business, 14–16, 23, 31, 44; children, interest in, 31; desk, 15; property, 47; resoluteness, 34, 36, 38; son, concern for, 7, 10–12, 14, 17, 23, 31, 44–45; son's marriage, 60; temper, 35; tidiness, 18; voice, 45
Audubon, Jean Jacques. *See* Audubon, John James
Audubon, John James: accuracy, 118–21, 139, 170; adventures, 78, 113; appearance, 123; artistry, 172; assets, 67; bird shooting, 52; birth, 7; birthday presents, 13; boyhood, 1–8; brother-in-law, *see* Bakewell, Thomas; build, 43; business affairs, 47, 59, 69–70, 75, 78, 92, 95–98, 104–05, 138; clothes, 5, 8, 53–54, 88, 105, 123, 145; common sense, 137; correspondence, 127; courage, 90; dancing, 24–25, 27–28, 35, 54; death, 177; debt, 105; disposition, 122; drawing, 21, 29, 51–52, 61, 84, 116; dreams, 40, 42–43, 90; dress, 5, 8, 53–54, 88, 105, 123, 145; eating, 27; enemies, 174; exploration, love of, 9–11; father, *see* Audubon, Captain; fatigue, 153; faults, 173; fellowships, 136; fencing, 26, 35; fever, 48; flattery of, 125; genius, 172; guardian, *see* Dacosta, Francis; hair, 123–24; health, 126; height, 53; hunting, 93; impracticality, 173; industry, 135, 172; integrity, 172; journals, 118, 121, 153, 174; Kentucky journey, 68–69; kindness, 174; Labrador journey, 164–68;

legends, 94; letters, 137, 153; life work, 75, 80–82, 96, 105–06, 115–16, 128, 137; marriage, 67; marriage plans, 60, 63; mathematics, 14, 20, 30, 47; mechanical drawing, 35; mind, 64; misfortunes, 105; mother, death, 7; music, 25, 93, 100–01; nature, collections, 18, 34, 61; nature, love of, 1–2, 4, 6, 12, 15–18, 20, 31, 153; nickname, 2; notes, 121; nurse, 8–9; painting and sketching, 13, 20–22, 105, 113, 117, 127, 139, 164; Paris sojourn, 38–44; people, meeting, 64; perfection, striving for, 82–86; perseverance, 137, 173; personality, 93; portfolio, 76, 86–87, 122–23, 138; portraits, 174–75; practical jokes, 102–03; "prudence", 135; purpose, singleness of, 80–81, 174; roaming, 52, 61, 108; room, 8, 13, 117; scalping, escape from, 92; schooling, 4, 12–13, 20–21, 31; self-confidence, 137; self-teaching, 84; shrewdness, 137; shyness, 36; skating, 54; sketching and painting, 13, 20–22, 105, 113, 117, 127, 139, 164; sobriety, 135; social life, 53–57, 127, 137; sons, *see* Audubon, John W., Audubon, Victor; spirits, 146, 154, 156; spoiled childhood, 1–8; stepmother, *see* Audubon, Madame; stepsister, *see* Audubon, Muguet; tardiness, 4; temper, 173; travels, 69, 115, 138; vanity, 173; violin, 35, 100–01, 114; walking, 47–48; wife, *see* Audubon, Lucy; wistfulness, 174
Audubon, John W., 96, 134, 142, 163–65, 176
udubon, Lucy Bakewell: burden, 145; clothes, 72; correspondence handling, 157–60; directness, 160; encouragement, 128–29, 147; family, 72; husband, belief in, 66, 72, 75, 80, 128–29, 133, 160; husband, love of, 57; husband, meeting, 56–57; marriage, 67; marriage plans, 60, 63; "rivals", 82; letters, 158–60; security, 72; serv-

179